Creating Learning Centered Classrooms
What Does Learning Theory Have to Say?

by Frances K. Stage, Patricia A. Muller, Jillian Kinzie, and Ada Simmons

ASHE-ERIC Higher Education Report Volume 26, Number 4

Prepared by

ERIC Clearinghouse on Higher Education
The George Washington University
URL: www.gwu.edu/~eriche

In cooperation with

Association for the Study
of Higher Education
URL: http://www.tiger.coe.missouri.edu/~ashe

Published by

WASHINGTON DC

Graduate School of Education and Human Development
The George Washington University
URL: www.gwu.edu

Jonathan D. Fife, Series Editor

Cite as

Stage, Frances K., Patricia A. Muller, Jillian Kinzie, and Ada Simmons. 1998. *Creating Learning Centered Classrooms: What Does Learning Theory Have to Say?* ASHE-ERIC Higher Education Report Volume 26, No. 4. Washington, D.C.: The George Washington University, Graduate School of Education and Human Development.

Library of Congress Catalog Card Number 98-85991
ISSN 0884-0040
ISBN 1-878380-84-2

Managing Editor: Lynne J. Scott
Manuscript Editor: Barbara Fishel/Editech
Cover Design by Michael David Brown, Inc., The Red Door Gallery, Rockport, ME

The ERIC Clearinghouse on Higher Education invites individuals to submit proposals for writing monographs for the *ASHE-ERIC Higher Education Report* series. Proposals must include:
1. A detailed manuscript proposal of not more than five pages.
2. A chapter-by-chapter outline.
3. A 75-word summary to be used by several review committees for the initial screening and rating of each proposal.
4. A vita and a writing sample.

ERIC Clearinghouse on Higher Education
Graduate School of Education and Human Development
The George Washington University
One Dupont Circle, Suite 630
Washington, DC 20036-1183

> *The mission of the ERIC system is to improve American education by increasing and facilitating the use of educational research and information on practice in the activities of learning, teaching, educational decision making, and research, wherever and whenever these activities take place.*

This publication was prepared partially with funding from the Office of Educational Research and Improvement, U.S. Department of Education, under contract no. ED RR-93-002008. The opinions expressed in this report do not necessarily reflect the positions or policies of OERI or the Department.

EXECUTIVE SUMMARY

The time is ripe for a closer examination of learning in college classrooms. Recent questioning of the value of higher education focuses on the worth of undergraduate education and on the quality of learning that takes place in college classrooms. In response, many colleges and universities have focused on changes that center on improving teaching and learning. In the past decade, we have seen a focus on teaching techniques in college classrooms, a movement that emphasizes active learning, the value of out-of-class learning, and the importance of assessment on college campuses. We have addressed the all-important issue of learning by college students without focusing on the all-important question of *how* our students learn academic material. One change that could begin to maximize students' learning would create "learning-centered" campuses (Barr and Tagg 1995). To create such a campus, we need to know how college students learn, to understand barriers to students' learning, and to develop classroom techniques that promote learning among college students. The keys to this knowledge lie in the fields of psychology, philosophy, and sociology; many have a basis in the study of children's learning and development, but we know much about the learning of youth and adults as well, particularly in academe.

What Theories and Frameworks Are Relevant to Learning in College?

Some of the many models of learning theories are particularly relevant to the traditional college classroom. For example, research shows that college students' attributions for success or failure (Weiner 1992) and their beliefs about their own abilities, or self-efficacy (Bandura 1997), influence students' motivation and goals for academic work. Moreover, some theories expand our view beyond the individual student and focus on the social context of learning. Approaches to learning that promote social constructivism, or learning within a social context, and that feature active group constructions of knowledge (Jaworski 1994) provide an ideal environment for some learners. Approaches to learning that create awareness of students' social conscience and that promote an awareness of possibilities for social transformation through action, such as conscientization (Freire and Faundez 1989), can stimulate learning, particularly for students from traditionally disadvantaged groups. And the theories of multiple intelligences (Gardner 1983) and learning styles (Kolb 1981) help us challenge timeworn assumptions about learners and learning that can exclude students and that limit our ways of thinking about the role of the college student in the classroom.

What Do We Know about College Students' Learning?
Research tells us much about learning in college; for example, we know that students can develop realistic attributions regarding success and failure that lead to positive study behaviors when working with counselors. Researchers have also demonstrated that constructs related to self-efficacy are positively related to achievement. And in several instances, classes designed for low-achieving students that focused on developing self-efficacy as well as academic learning experienced dramatic successes. Social constructivist approaches to learning have been applied through classroom practices such as collaborative learning, problem-based learning, and peer learning groups. Most often, students who participate in these innovative instructional approaches perceive a more meaningful learning experience and in some cases actually learn more than students in conventional learning situations. Research on the application of Freire's theory of conscientization is more limited, and scholars are only beginning to apply the theory with nontraditional students and in ESL (English as a second language) courses. With regard to theories of learning styles and multiple intelligences, researchers have validated the existence of the various ways of learning and the existence of various types of intelligence. Many examples of ways to apply the theories in the classroom are available.

What Practices Promote Learning Among College Students?
From the literature focusing on frameworks and theories of learning, we can identify several general practices that promote learning for college students:

- Social learning experiences, such as peer teaching and group projects, particularly those that promote group construction of knowledge, allow a student to observe other students model successful learning, and encourage him or her to emulate them (social constructivism, self-efficacy, learning styles);
- Varying instructional models that deviate from the lecture format, such as visual presentations, site visits, and use of

the Internet (multiple intelligences, learning styles, self-efficacy);

- Varying expectations for students' performance, from individual written formats to group work that includes writing and presentation, interpretation of theatrical, dance, musical, or artistic work, and performance of actual tasks at a work site (attribution theory, conscientization, multiple intelligences, learning styles);
- Choices that allow students to capitalize on personal strengths and interests (self-efficacy, multiple intelligences, learning styles);
- Overt use of sociocultural situations and methods that provide authentic contexts and enculturation into an academic disciplinary community (social constructivism, conscientization);
- Course material that demonstrates valuing of diverse cultures, ethnic groups, classes, and genders (conscientization, learning styles).

Although it might be difficult or even impossible to incorporate all these practices into one college class, if most college classes could incorporate just a few of these elements, colleges would develop into more learning-centered communities and would move toward meeting the learning needs of a greater portion of their students.

What Additional Questions Must Be Answered?
Many important questions about college students' learning remain to be explored through research. Although we know that students' beliefs and attributions affect learning, we are not sure whether an instructor can apply techniques that will modify those beliefs and attributions to help students learn. And although literature exists to describe innovations in the classroom designed to foster learning using various models and theories, few authors have systematically tracked differences in learning across classes. Such research is needed to establish definitively the importance of these theories and models. Finally, differences in learning by gender and across racial subgroups need to be explored. Carefully designed studies employing both quantitative and naturalistic approaches are needed to help us learn more about these important topics.

CONTENTS

FOREWORD

The paradigm of college teaching and student learning has evolved measurably over the past two decades. In the 1970s and 1980s, the teaching/learning model all too frequently included professors whose training in teaching consisted primarily of experiencing good and bad teachers as they developed in-depth knowledge in their intellectual specialty. Having little or no training in teaching, professors used the pedagogical skills that were the most effective in their own learning. Thus did past practices beget future practices: A student who is lectured at becomes a professor who lectures to. This concept of "the sage on the stage" is exemplified by the professor who began his class by saying, "My job is to talk and your job is to listen, and let us hope we both conclude our jobs at the same time."

This model of developing college faculty began to come under attack in the mid-1980s when graduate students who were teaching assistants began to receive some formal training to develop their teaching skills. Even in the late 1990s, however, the majority of students graduating with doctoral degrees have had little or no formal training to develop their teaching skills and little or no exposure to the research on teaching and learning.

Teaching styles, on the other hand, have received more and more attention at the national meetings of higher education associations. In particular, the lecture style—involving active teaching and passive learning—has been severely questioned. The concept of active learning, with faculty and students participating together as they develop an understanding of the subject matter, has received much more attention, both in the literature and at conference workshops.

The emphasis on scrutinizing the effectiveness of various teaching styles to promote greater learning is now evolving to greater attention and emphasis on learning itself. In 1998, the theme of the American Association for Higher Education conference was "taking learning seriously." This change in emphasis is a major shift in the teaching/learning model. Essentially, it acknowledges that the success of education depends on how much a student is learning, and it acknowledges that the teacher's success depends on how well the professor's teaching style and the student's learning style fit.

The authors of *Creating Learning Centered Classrooms: What Does Learning Theory Have to Say?*—Frances K. Stage, professor of educational leadership and policy studies,

Patricia A. Muller, research associate for the Indiana Center for Evaluation, Jillian Kinzie, research associate, and Ada Simmons, research analyst in the Office of the Vice Chancellor for Academic Affairs, all at Indiana University—focus on this underemphasized part of the teaching/learning equation, carefully examine the frameworks that have been established for the college classroom, and review the research and theories that relate to students' learning. They examine attribution theory, college students' self-efficacy, social constructivism, and Freire's theory of conscientization, and review the theories that either support or refute popular assumptions about the college classroom. The authors conclude by offering five specific practices for the classroom that promote greater learning for college students.

The shift from an emphasis on the quality of teaching to an emphasis on the quality of learning is significant, because it is also a shift in professional orientation for the faculty. When the emphasis is on teaching, too often the professional attitude toward learning outcomes is blame: "I taught well, but they didn't bother to take the time to learn well." Therefore, a student's poor performance is the student's fault. When the emphasis is on students' learning, however, faculty and students begin to share responsibility for learning, and the faculty's professionalism is measured by the learning success of the classroom. *Creating Learning Centered Classrooms* helps to develop the knowledge base that faculty need to promote this partnership in teaching and learning.

Jonathan D. Fife
Series Editor,
Professor of Higher Education Administration, and
Director, ERIC Clearinghouse on Higher Education

Approximately 53 percent of students at four-year institutions and 68 percent of students at community colleges drop out during their first year (Ratcliff and Associates 1995).

Of women students in the top 10 percent of SAT scores, fewer than half describe themselves as in the top 10 percent. After four years of college, fewer than a quarter describe themselves as in the top 10 percent (Drew 1996).

Science students with positive attitudes toward science were less positive after taking a traditional botany course; nonscience majors with more negative initial attitudes were more positive after taking an introductory anatomy and physiology course stressing relevancy and high-interest activities (Gogolin and Swartz 1992).

These statistics and others have raised alarm on college campuses. Assumptions that learning automatically occurs in association with attending college have largely disappeared. We are no longer assured that by the time students reach college, success is imminent. And we have grown beyond viewing academic failure in college as a pathology of students that implied either a problem with selection (the student never should have been admitted in the first place) or socialization (competing interests and demands interfered with a student's focus on academic matters). Only recently, however, have actual classroom-related experiences been critically examined for their relevance to college students' success.

Extensive work in the study of college students has related social processes to college students' success (Pascarella and Terenzini 1991). In recent decades, however, little attempt was made to connect those processes to individual characteristics, despite constant urging for a focus on individuals with regard to motivation (Cross 1976; Stage 1989) and cognitive styles and academic learning (Svinicki 1990). Through the early 1980s, most individually focused work concentrated on issues of personal decision making and development. With few exceptions (Light 1990, 1992; Menges and Svinicki 1991; Menges, Weimer, and Associates 1996), not many in higher education have examined how college students learn and the extent to which theories of learning, for the most part grounded in precollege education, can be extended to students in college classrooms. The time for a closer examination of learning theories could not be more appropriate, however, as educational critics, legislators, prospective employers, and consumers all call for empirical evidence of students' learning and acquired skills associated with college attendance (American Association 1992; Gardiner 1994). Applying theories of student learning to college classrooms can enhance the conditions for learning and, it is hoped, result in educational gains.

A recent decade of intensive focus on teaching styles and methods, but largely ignoring learning, has led higher education leaders to the conclusion that a focus merely on instruction is one-sided. Currently, efforts are being made to create a more balanced discourse that emphasizes the subtle nuances and complexities of learning within any discussion of teaching (Barr and Tagg 1995; Love and Love 1995; Travis 1995). In fact, some suggest shifting from an instructional paradigm in higher education that focuses on increasing and improving instruction to a learning paradigm that emphasizes enhancing students' learning (Barr and Tagg 1995). In a learning paradigm, we no longer presume that every student learns the same way or that widely accepted teaching practices necessarily result in optimal levels of learning for students (Barr and Tagg 1995; Guskin 1997; Rendon 1994; Rhoads and Valadez 1996; Stage and Manning 1992; Tierney 1993). Taking a learning-centered perspective, scholars increasingly regard the classroom as a dynamic setting where pedagogical practices and learners' characteristics meet and where the quality of this interaction influences outcomes that were formerly presumed to occur in college classrooms (Barr and Tagg 1995; Menges and Svinicki 1991; Millar 1996; Palmer 1993, 1997). Interest in these dynamics has increased, but with the exception of a few authors, much current literature on college students' learning and college teaching is largely atheoretical, from a psychological standpoint. The frameworks discussed in this monograph expand conceptual thinking and extend theoretical issues to a discussion of a learning-centered college campus.

Why Frameworks of Learning?
The purpose of this monograph is to bring selected frameworks of learning to the attention of faculty and administra-

tors. These frameworks, predominantly from psychology but from philosophy and sociology as well, have existed for decades and have been incorporated into primary and secondary education but for a number of reasons have not been so widely embraced by those who instruct and support college students. First, college faculty are typically not schooled in pedagogy and consequently may not be familiar with psychological and sociological frameworks that underpin effective pedagogy. Nor do the vast majority typically read teaching literature after their faculty careers have been launched. Second, tinkering with teaching can be a risky proposition. The lecture format, in which the faculty member is regarded as the sole authority, is a long-standing model in higher education. Changes to the status quo on either side of the teaching/learning equation can be threatening for faculty and for students, and the results at times can be unpredictable or disappointing. Finally, teaching and learning have been regarded as separate processes. Traditional expectations for the classroom place responsibility for teaching squarely on faculty and responsibility for learning squarely on students.

Limiting the choice of topics to the scope of this volume was difficult. Some recent literature on the learning of college students takes a functional rather than a theoretical view. For example, much work on college students' learning focuses on learning outside the classroom and institution-wide climate and activities. Other literature focuses on specific learning strategies, such as active learning and collaborative learning. This monograph focuses on frameworks that relate most closely to academic learning and relates those frameworks to current practices of teaching and learning. Thus, theories and models were chosen that help us understand important differences between students as they react to, resonate toward, and interpret academic activities. Another criterion for selecting frameworks was to choose those that could be readily incorporated by faculty as they conceive of their approach to teaching and construct their classes and class-related activities. "Good teaching" covers nearly an infinite variety of styles, students, and subject matter, and the materials presented here reflect that variety. A final criterion was a desire to focus on theories that might be unfamiliar to many readers. Omissions of theories are the result of practical considerations and do not imply a judgment of unworthiness or a lack of interest.

These frameworks have existed for decades but for a number of reasons have not been so widely embraced by those who instruct and support college students.

This monograph is intended to serve as a primary resource for those whose interest, whether professional or academic, is in academic learning on the college campus. College faculty will find the suggestions for enhancing learning, as well as the frameworks behind those suggestions, useful as they conceive their classes. Professionals, such as academic advisers and faculty development specialists, may find frameworks of learning useful as they formulate partnerships across departments and administrative units to reinforce learning in the classroom. And researchers and students of higher education will find useful discussions of college classroom phenomena as well as possibilities for their own research on college students' learning.

The frameworks covered in this volume differ from psychological theories more typically associated with the literature on college students. Those theories and models usually focus on college students' personal development (as opposed to learning) and include foci on tasks (Chickering 1969; Heath 1968), characteristics of learners (Holland 1985; Myers 1980), decision making, attitudes about learning, and intellectual development (Baxter-Magolda 1990; Gilligan 1982; Kitchener and King 1990; W. Perry 1981), and involvement in college activities (A. Astin 1984; Blake 1985; Kuh, Schuh, Whitt, and Associates 1991; Pace 1979, 1990).

As we wrote, we envisioned faculty in "traditional college classrooms." New approaches to instruction, such as on-line and interactive video education and courses in the workplace, are mentioned in conjunction with some theories, but full discussion of the scope and usefulness of such innovation would fill a second monograph. This volume is meant to complement books that focus on teaching and on college students' intellectual development. Selected frameworks are introduced briefly, relevant research presented, and implications for learning in the college classroom discussed. Rather than presenting theory in a seeming vacuum devoid of historical context, we begin with a brief overview of, first, cognitive science and, second, motivation. The task is enormous, so more interested readers are urged to consult references cited in each section.

Overview
A behaviorist view of humans and their interactions with the world dominated psychological theories through much of this century. B.F. Skinner (1953, 1968), one well-known

theorist, believed the goal of psychology was to predict and control behavior. Following the mainstream social science tradition of the scientific method, learning was often studied within carefully controlled experimental settings that were frequently far removed from the complex realities of actual learning. And thought, motivation, emotions, culture, and environment were viewed as irrelevant. The influence of behaviorist theory is still evident today in teaching and learning on the college campus in classroom emphases on drill and practice, habit breaking, and attention to the consequences of behavior (Ormrod 1990).

Behaviorist views of learning have been criticized for being too linear, causal, and simplistic. In contrast to the ideas of behaviorists, some theorists take cognitive and sociocultural approaches to learning. During the last part of this century, the discipline of educational psychology focused heavily on cognitive functioning and on how people process, organize, and retrieve information. Other scholars emphasized the importance of social learning and criticized cognitive approaches that ignored context and treated learners as largely biological organisms (Bandura 1977; Bandura and Walters 1963). These writers promoted constructs of sociocultural learning described in the early decades of the 20th century (Vygotsky 1978). As a result, the context in which learning takes place has taken on increased significance within these cognitive frameworks. Many psychologists believe that "knowledge in human memory seems to be 'stored' in contextual fashion" (Glover, Ronning, and Bruning 1990, p. 23). This work was an important precursor to current approaches to learning (several of which are discussed in this monograph) that emphasize the importance of mentoring, modeling roles for instructors and students, and internships in the academic context.

Many researchers agree that some students have difficulty taking knowledge learned in one type of setting and applying it in another (see Glover, Ronning, and Bruning 1990 and Slavin 1997 for further discussion). For college students, learning often occurs embedded in the context of a classroom, and students may struggle when they attempt to translate that learning into job-related activities and decision making. Classroom activities that represent the complexity of decision making in the "real world" are rare. But educators can enhance the learning process by structuring such activities inside and outside the classroom. For example, internships and classroom assignments can provide contexts within which students are able to interpret and apply what they learned in the classroom. Learning processes developed in coordination with the curriculum, such as service-learning experiences, can also contribute extensively to learning. By providing contexts for learning, faculty can help create experiences that give structure and meaning to learning in the classroom for college students. Frameworks described later in this monograph provide the rationale for incorporating such experiences in the college curriculum.

Similarly, motivational theories are recognized as critical in understanding behavior and learning (McKeachie, Pintrich, Lin, Smith, and Sharma 1990). Motivation is defined as "an internal process that activates, guides, and maintains behavior over time" (Slavin 1997, p. 345). An attempt to describe motivation established a hierarchy of needs that motivates humans (Maslow 1954). According to the theory, needs at one level must be somewhat satisfied before an individual is motivated to satisfy higher-level needs. The first levels, *physiological needs* (food, drink, sex, and shelter) and *safety needs* (security, order, protection, and family stability), are often taken for granted but can sometimes interfere with college students' pursuit of higher-level needs. The next two, *love needs* (affection, group affiliation, and personal acceptance) and *esteem needs* (self-respect, prestige, reputation, and social status), are likely to be central to college students' lives. Moreover, according to Maslow, these two types of needs must be somewhat satisfied before an individual begins to focus on *self-actualization needs* (self-fulfillment and achievement of lifetime personal goals).

Generally in higher education, motivation has been used as a global measure within sociological models used to describe students' satisfaction or success in college (Pascarella 1985; Stage 1989; Weidman 1989). In fact, some researchers assume that merely by enrolling in college, a student has demonstrated motivation. Most who work with college students know differently. Often motivation seems and is treated as an immutable characteristic as fixed as a demographic description; those with motivation succeed, those without do not. Studies of motivation in the context of the college classroom are rarer (but see Forsyth and McMillan 1991, McMillan and Forsyth 1991, and Pintrich 1989 for examples). And a few authors have provided descriptions of methods for changing motivation (see Forsyth and McMillan 1991; Matthews 1996; R. Perry, Menec, and Struthers 1996; Slavin 1997). Yet motivation remains an almost mystifying force in success in college. From motivation in general, the discussion moves to specific behaviors in the classroom. Two of the frameworks described in this monograph, attribution and self-efficacy, illuminate aspects of this perplexing construct that are particularly useful in considering academic learning. Other aspects of motivation, such as anxiety, expectancy/values, and goal setting (not covered in this book), can also help us understand the concept.

Motivational theorists have also focused on the role that intrinsic goals play in learning and development. College students who develop their own internal goals for learning, aside from any official or familial coercion, are more likely to succeed, whether inside or outside the classroom. For students who have academic difficulty, efforts that focus on learning skills and test anxiety and that seek to help students match their learning experiences with their personal goals are obvious ways that motivation might be positively influenced.

Some theorists and researchers describe motivation in terms of two components: the *perceived probability of success* and the *incentive value of success* (Slavin 1997). In other words, if a student perceives a high probability of success but does not value the activity, he or she is unlikely to be motivated to participate. On the other hand, if a student values an activity but perceives a low probability of success, he or she is similarly unmotivated. Perceived probability of success is closely related to individuals' beliefs about self and self-efficacy (Pajares 1996). Expectancy-value has been found to be related to college students' engagement in various activities (Eccles 1994; Stewart and Roach 1993; Sullins et al. 1995). A review of theories of teaching and learning takes an expectation approach to motivation (McKeachie et al. 1990), describing a complex web of relationships among students' goals, perceived value of learning tasks, students' efficacy at learning tasks, test anxiety, and expected outcomes, all of which are related to students' motivation.*

―――――
*These summaries are intended to establish only the briefest context for discussion of the frameworks presented in this monograph. Readers interested in learning more about the topics of motivation and cognitive science are urged to consult any of the sources mentioned in this section, particularly Glover, Ronning, and Bruning 1990, Hilgard 1987, McKeachie et al. 1990, and Slavin 1997.

Organization of This Volume

The remainder of this monograph highlights the frameworks judged to hold particular relevance for understanding academic learning at the college level. The description of frameworks is by no means exhaustive, and many other learning theories still need to be examined for their relevance to college students' learning. Readers may note, within the characterizations, overlapping observations by diverse scholars. These similarities serve to highlight aspects of learning that are pervasive and important. It is hoped that readers find these frameworks (as well as their overlapping principles) useful as they create learning environments on their own college campuses.

The first part of the monograph covers particular frameworks in detail. The next two sections cover two important personal aspects of motivation, performance attribution and self-efficacy. The two sections following, which cover social constructivism and conscientization, represent a shift from the individual to a social perspective and highlight two frameworks that place more emphasis on the sociocultural contexts of learning and the social construction of knowledge. Each section uses a case study to detail elements of the theoretical construct, briefly outline relevant research on young adult and college student populations, describe relationships of the frameworks to college students' learning, and discuss possible educational applications. "Other Theories: Challenging Classroom Assumptions" describes several additional frameworks more briefly. They are particularly useful for challenging assumptions about learning and identifying factors that might inhibit learning for college students.

The second part of the monograph focuses on the usefulness of these frameworks for studying and engendering academic learning. "A Need for Classroom-Based Research" discusses the limited research on learning in the classroom for college students and identifies particular research needed. "Implications for the College Classroom" relates particular approaches to learning to the frameworks from the earlier sections, emphasizing the importance of diverse methods for presenting academic material, various activities to facilitate learning, and multiple ways for students to demonstrate their learning. The concluding section discusses these frameworks' relevance to current and future academic issues.

A conscientious student, Carolyn kept up with her calculus coursework, monitored her understanding of course material, and devoted regular and systematic study time to her schoolwork. Her diligence in studying had paid off with good grades in high school, and Carolyn looked forward to a college major in chemistry as a gateway to a medical career. By the fourth week of class in her freshman year of college, however, she was feeling a little panicky about calculus. In class, the professor moved rapidly through problems, and when Carolyn missed a step, she got flustered and couldn't follow the remainder of the explanation.

Carolyn began to suspect that a lack of aptitude in math must be preventing her from grasping the material when it was presented in class, because she had always had to study more for math than her other subjects. Her attempts to review the material outside class were also unsuccessful, because her class notes were sketchy in spots where she had paused to reflect on a puzzling part of the solution to a problem and overly detailed when she became confused and could no longer distinguish trivial information from more critical points. Self-consciousness about her perceived lack of ability kept her from scheduling extra sessions with her instructor or classmates. By the end of each class session, Carolyn was frustrated and upset, and her apprehension built as the day of her calculus final examination approached.

Despite regular class attendance and lengthy study time, Carolyn had received a barely passing grade on the midterm exam, reinforcing her suspicion that her aptitude in math was weak. Discouraged, she decided to hedge her academic bets, reducing her study time on calculus and devoting more to classes where she felt effort would pay off with higher grades. A low grade on the calculus final seemed to confirm her suspicion that she lacked the ability to succeed in college-level math courses, and soon after the exam, Carolyn dropped the follow-up mathematics course she had registered for and began to consider changing her academic major to one that required less math.

According to attribution theorists, when Carolyn unexpectedly performed poorly in her college calculus course, she was likely to engage in a cognitive process termed "causal search." In causal search, individuals try to understand *why* events have happened or what motives have directed the actions of others. By connecting outcomes to causes, Carolyn can reduce the stress associated with uncertainty and understand herself better (Weiner 1986, 1992). Moreover, the conclusions that Carolyn reaches about herself and her environment through causal search have important implications for her achievement motivation, learning, and future academic performance (Licht and Dweck 1983).

By midcentury, Kelly (1955), Heider (1958), and other attributional theorists had begun to redirect attention away from explaining achievement behavior by how people *feel* to what people *believe* (Covington 1992). In particular, Fritz Heider (1958), the founding father of attribution theory, is credited with defining many of the basic issues, including the notion that to understand why someone behaves as he or she does, we must first establish the causality of the behavior as internal to the individual, external in the environment, or both. This section defines the key principles of attribution theory, explains the connections between attributions and motivation to learn, and draws implications for college students and those who teach and counsel them.

Causal Search in Learning Contexts
What situations prompt causal search? Causal search typically is not undertaken for routine occurrences but is reserved for unexpected outcomes, nonattainment of goals, or in situations that have important personal implications (Hastie 1984). Unexpected failure at an important event is especially likely to elicit causal thinking (Weiner 1986). Because Carolyn was a successful student in high school who apparently had had no difficulties with mathematics, it seems likely that her near-failure would have prompted a causal search. Causal search is neither mechanical nor straightforward, and people may differ in their causal explanations for events despite having undergone similar circumstances and experienced identical outcomes. In the example described above, Carolyn could have drawn other conclusions about her failure with calculus. People pay attention to different pieces of information in their environment and interpret the meaning of this information differently, which can lead to alternative explanations for similar events. Because Carolyn's failure was inconsistent

with her past record of success with mathematics and other subjects, her explanation of low ability for her low grades is somewhat surprising (Weiner 1992). Some evidence suggests, however, that females, especially bright females, are more inclined to draw negative conclusions about their ability (particularly in mathematics) and are more debilitated after failure than other students (Eccles, Adler, Futterman, Goff, Kaczala, Meece, and Midgley 1983; Ryckman and Peckham 1987; Stipek and Hoffman 1980), a point discussed later. Whether or not it seems to others to be warranted, Carolyn's attribution diminished her motivation to achieve in mathematics and redirected her immediate and long-term academic and career plans. We now take a closer look at the process explaining how this situation happens and what can be done to reverse it.

Within achievement domains, empirical studies suggest that the range of salient explanations for outcomes is surprisingly narrow, with ability and effort predominating (Weiner 1986). Apparently, humans rely on a simplistic scheme of two factors in accounting for achievement-related activities: how competent we are and how hard we try. Competitive classroom situations emphasize and reward ability (or competence) over effort, making it very important for students to protect and advance images of their ability to themselves and others to maintain self-esteem (Covington 1992). Because of our natural self-protective human nature and classroom conditions that encourage social comparison rather than mastery of the subject, students typically exhibit self-serving attributional bias in which they tend to take credit for academic successes by claiming internal factors (for example, effort or ability) and distance themselves from failure by placing fault on factors in the environment (such as a difficult task or bad luck) (Anazonwu 1995; Basow and Medcalf 1988; DeBoer 1985; Stipek 1984). In some instances, these tendencies might reflect overly optimistic self-assessment if not outright self-deception, traits that have their own set of associated pitfalls. On the other hand, self-serving attributional bias generates in individuals the motivation to try again with more effort after failure rather than decrease effort and give up. In the final analysis, our attributional biases may work in our favor to facilitate the further development of our abilities.

Causal search involves more than simply identifying the perceived cause of success or failure. Of more critical impor-

Some evidence suggests, however, that females, especially bright females, are more inclined to draw negative conclusions about their ability and are more debilitated after failure than other students.

tance is how the cause itself is classified on three underlying dimensions: control, stability, and locus. These dimensions appear to hold across a broad range of situations and motivational contexts (Weiner 1986). Although each dimension can be conceptualized as continua spanning from one extreme to the other, researchers typically assign causal attributions into discrete, bipolar categories: controllable versus uncontrollable, stable versus unstable, internal versus external (Weiner 1979). The dimension of controllability distinguishes whether a cause is under volitional control, that is, whether an individual can increase or decrease it by effort. Stability refers to whether a cause fluctuates or remains relatively constant. The dimension of locus defines whether the outcome is contingent on internal factors within the individual or external in the environment (Weiner 1986). Each of the three underlying dimensions influences a different aspect of motivation. The dimensions of controllability and locus relate more to affective consequences of success and failure, such as pride, self-esteem, shame, and guilt. The dimension of stability influences an individual's expectancy of future success following a success or failure. Given the centrality of the concept of expectancy to attribution theory and several other motivation theories, detailed discussion in this section is limited to the dimension of stability. With these definitions and the basic attributional principles established, we now explore how motivation and learning are affected by causal attributions and the dimensions that underlie them.

Causal Attributions and Motivation

As mentioned, ability and effort are typically cited as causes for academic outcomes. Although they are both classified as internal factors, let us consider their differential effects on motivation by more closely examining their differences on the dimension of stability. In the event of success achieved under stable conditions, high expectations for future success are maintained. Thus, an individual who believes both that ability is responsible for past success and that ability is a stable trait* will most likely expect success on similar tasks

*Although ability is typically classified in attribution schemes as a stable trait, evidence suggests that individuals may be of two minds on the matter. A considerable body of research continues to develop around the perceived nature of intelligence (that is, whether it is regarded as basically stable or changeable) and the effects of these perceptions on motivation and learning.

in the future (Weiner 1979, 1986). Self-esteem and motivation remain high. Expectancy of future success may be somewhat reduced, however, when previous successes are attributed to effort, because most people perceive effort to be a variable trait.*

Expectancies for future success are likely to be highest when successes are attributed to ability, but a balanced interpretation has some benefits. As students use cognitive strategies to solve problems at hand and attribute their successes to their efforts, they gain confidence that they can, in the future, apply their intellect and learned skills to help them successfully complete unfamiliar challenging tasks. When problem-solving situations arise in the future, they are more likely to use the cognitive tools at their disposal (Borkowski, Carr, Rellinger, and Pressley 1990). On the other hand, the converse is also true: Failure to make the connection between personal ability and effort, and performance outcomes may negatively affect learning by retarding development of an individual's ability to effectively marshal intellectual and emotional resources to attack academic tasks (Carr, Borkowski, and Maxwell 1991).

The dynamics of causal attribution operate the same way for failures as they do for successes, but the changes to expectancy, self-efficacy, and self-esteem are in the opposite direction. When failure is attributed to stable, uncontrollable causes such as ability, it is frequently accompanied by a low sense of self-efficacy (Abramson, Garber, and Seligman 1980; Schunk 1982), and motivation is diminished because future performance cannot be expected to improve. Drops in expectancy are most drastic after failure ascribed to stable causes such as ability, even among college students (DeBoer 1985). In fact, the more one ascribes failure to low ability, the lower expectancy, perceived competence, and persistence (Weiner 1992). Continual attributions of failure to stable, uncontrollable factors can also lead to the reduction of effort on challenging tasks (Weiner 1986, 1992), unproductive strategies for seeking academic help (Ames and Lau 1982; Nelson-LeGall 1985), the adoption of passive coping strategies (C. Peterson

---

*Again, some students may consider effort to be relatively invariant because of a regular pattern of hard work and subsequent success in achievement. In this case, they are likely to maintain high expectations for future success, presuming they also believe that the conditions that enabled them to work hard remain stable for the future.

and Barrett 1987), and reduced intentions of pursuing further coursework in the academic area of failure (DeBoer 1985). Eventually, students may simply quit trying as a result of low expectations for future success. Unfortunately, Carolyn, our hypothetical student struggling with calculus, fits this profile remarkably well. Her interpretation of the cause of her poor performance had far-reaching effects—on the amount and quality of effort she was willing to spend on mastering the subject, on her willingness to avail herself of academic support services, on her ability to cognitively process material both in and out of class, and eventually on her academic plans.

When failure is attributed to unstable or controllable causes, such as insufficient effort, students do not usually believe that future failures are inevitable. Research provides empirical verification that students who make low-effort attributions for failure are more likely than students who attribute failure to controllable or invariant causes to maintain high expectations for future successes. Expectancy remains high because their perceptions of personal ability have been preserved by claiming low effort as the cause of failure (Anderson and Jennings 1980; Diener and Dweck 1980). Following failure, they are also more likely to increase their effort compared with students who attributed their failure to uncontrollable causes and, consequently, may be more effective at solving the problem at hand and improving their future performance (Diener and Dweck 1980). When a student claims low effort caused failure, the contribution of ability to the outcome is unclear and self-esteem is protected, a psychological outcome that is more likely to encourage motivation and sustained effort on achievement tasks than attributing failure to low ability. Although authorities generally concur that attributing failure to effort is psychologically more adaptive than attributing failure to stable or uncontrollable factors on a singular instance, a pattern of attributing negative outcomes to low effort is considered maladaptive, as students may resist taking advantage of academic support or counseling in lieu of simply "trying harder" next time. In addition, when students regularly question their capacity to sustain effort, they are likely to become discouraged from persisting at difficult tasks (Schmitz and Skinner 1993).

Unfortunately, sometimes failure occurs even though a great deal of effort has been expended. Feelings of personal dissatisfaction and public shame, as well as attributing performance to insufficient ability, are typically strongest in these situations (Covington and Omelich 1979, 1981). Because low effort is no longer a plausible cause for failure, ability is suspect. In some situations, particularly at the lower grades, trying hard, even when a student fails, can benefit a student, because teachers' evaluations of a student's performance following failure are often softened by a show of effort. Because faculty are typically unaware of or unswayed by effort alone, however, college students may be in a quandary regarding effort. Although it is a formidable weapon against failure, effort can be the proverbial double-edged sword, turning against its master when failure occurs (Covington and Omelich 1979).

One way to avoid the damaging consequences to self-esteem of attributing failure to low ability is simply to deliberately exert low effort, as is the case with classic underachievers. Although students indicate that they would not do so, they suggest that others may purposefully disengage from expending effort on learning tasks in the interest of maintaining self-worth (Jagacinski and Nicholls 1990). Partying the night before a big test, for instance, may provide a ready excuse for poor performance without the damaging blows of having to claim lack of ability as a cause of failure. "Self-handicappers" do their best to divert attention away from low ability as an explanation for failure. The ideal self-handicapping strategy is one that imposes only a minimal impediment to success while simultaneously protecting self-esteem (Arkin and Baumgardner 1985). Procrastination and spreading oneself too thin are other examples of self-handicapping strategies that can lead to failure "with honor"—or at least one without disgrace (Covington 1992). Perhaps Carolyn, whose failure with calculus introduced this section, prematurely reduced her effort to avoid the stigma of trying and failing.

Less frequently, students attribute failure to external causes, such as bad luck or ineffective instruction. When failure is occasionally ascribed to chance or luck, the instability of these factors suggests a low expectancy for recurrence, and therefore expectancy for future success remains relatively high. When individuals continually attribute failure to external causes, however, they come to believe that their behaviors are unrelated to, or disconnected from, outcomes, and a sense of powerlessness about academic outcomes develops (Abramson, Garber, and Seligman 1980). Even when success occurs, such students typically take no personal credit. In the relationship between attributional beliefs and subsequent achievement, it is possible that attributional beliefs "drive" or "energize" students' capabilities for intellectual processing as well as the strategies they are willing and able to use for planning, modifying, and monitoring their learning (Borkowski and Thorpe 1994). Thus, in the presence of maladaptive beliefs, such as "helpless" patterns of response to academic challenge, cognitive capabilities are reduced, resulting in declines in subsequent performance (Borkowski and Thorpe 1994; Dweck and Licht 1980).

Continually attributing failure to unknown causes may be most damaging of all, because doing so indicates a global sense of confusion and loss of control over outcomes. Such conditions may lead to disaffection in the classroom and academic failure (Schmitz and Skinner 1993).

Relating Attributions to Other Motivational Concepts
Links between attributional beliefs and other motivation-related constructs, such as students' self-efficacy (Schunk 1982) and their ability to employ reasonable strategies to learning tasks (Borkowski and Thorpe 1994), have also been established. When students believe they control success, either because of their ability or their effort, their sense of efficacy relevant to their learning is reinforced and/or advanced (Relich, Debus, and Walker 1986; Schunk 1982). In turn, they are more inclined to monitor their levels of learning and the strategies they employ to bring about that learning (Borkowski and Thorpe 1994). So important are attributional beliefs to the development of healthy psychological attitudes toward learning that "in children, the entire system suffers when . . . attributional beliefs do not develop in concert with intellectual or academic achievements" (Borkowski and Thorpe 1994, p. 59). More generally, attributional beliefs play a central role in the formation of a relatively stable self-concept of ability (Eccles et al. 1983). In fact, it is self-concept rather than attributional beliefs that drive achievement behavior, while attributions merely mirror self-concept (Eccles et al. 1983). Regardless of the theoretical perspective one prefers, however, the role of causal attributions for success and failure in achievement behaviors is clear.

Gender Differences in Causal Attributions Regarding Achievement

A great deal of effort went into investigating gender differences in causal attributions for achievement during the late 1970s and early 1980s, as evidenced by studies documenting both the lack of and existence of gender differences in attributions for success and failure. Among studies that showed a difference in causal attribution patterns between males and females, women most often displayed the more maladaptive style, although the actual magnitude of the differences was seldom large (Frieze, Whitley, Hanusa, and McHugh 1982; Sohn 1982). Gender differences, if they exist, may be most notable between males and females who have a strong feminine sex-role orientation, or on tasks that are perceived as more appropriate for one gender or the other (McHugh, Frieze, and Hanusa 1982). For example, Carolyn, in the case presented earlier, probably was influenced by popular but untrue notions that women are predisposed to poor performance in mathematics. Additionally, females may have lower expectations with regard to achievement than males despite past records of success (Eccles et al. 1983; Licht and Dweck 1983; Stipek and Gralinski 1991; Vollmer 1986) and may be more inclined than males to both accept negative information and discount positive information about themselves (Dweck and Licht 1980). Furthermore, throughout the college years, male students typically rate their abilities more highly than females rate theirs (A. Astin 1993). These characteristics may help to account for the attributional tendencies of women, compared with men, to place more weight on lack of ability as a cause of failure and less weight on high ability as a cause of success (Fennema 1981; Parsons, Meece, Adler, and Kaczala 1982; Simmons 1996). Whether these findings would be upheld for females of racial minorities is unclear, because most prior research on the topic has been based on predominantly white samples.

The Formation of Causal Attributions

Understanding the factors that influence the formation of causal attributions reveals how faculty and other educators help shape students' attributions and work with students whose attributions are maladaptive.

Causal attributions are formed by the influence of antecedent cues, causal principles such as self-serving attributional bias, and current contextual cues (Weiner 1992). Antecedent cues typically include enduring beliefs and prior history of performance. In the absence of environmental cues that point to an obvious explanation, students fall back on their preferred attributional style, a relatively enduring perspective for interpreting outcomes of events. Intuitively and empirically, evidence exists that a pessimistic attribution style is associated with negative performance outcomes (Henry, Martinko, and Pierce 1993; C. Peterson 1990; C. Peterson and Barrett 1987; Pierce and Henry 1993). Current contextual cues include the amount of effort expended, the difficulty of the task, social norms such as the performance of peers on identical or similar tasks, and teachers' attributional cues communicated through comments and behaviors.

Several studies illustrate the role faculty can have in providing the sort of attributional feedback to students most likely to create conditions favorable to the development of healthy cognitive patterns.

Several studies illustrate the role faculty can have in providing the sort of attributional feedback to students most likely to create conditions favorable to the development of healthy cognitive patterns of taking credit for academic success and failure. In an experimental study involving younger students deficient in subtraction skills, instruction plus periodic verbal feedback linking successful problem solving with ability produced the largest gains in self-efficacy and skills, surpassing those of the no-feedback group, the effort-plus-ability group, and the effort-feedback group (Schunk 1982). The same results can be encouraged in college classrooms through the natural exchanges of conversation between faculty and students. As students struggle to interpret their academic performance, faculty can redirect students' disclaimers of ability for success and, likewise, their claims of low ability for failure. Without being inauthentic, faculty can express confidence to students that they possess the intellectual capital to succeed in college, and that discouraging achievement outcomes can be lessened by applying more effort or alternative strategies for mastering course material. Moreover, they can assist students in identifying and practicing the use of discipline-specific strategies that are most likely to bring academic success.

Faculty may question how much influence they can actually have on students' attributions. A study predicting first-year college students' internal attributions for their academic successes identified several instructional behaviors of faculty (Pascarella, Edison, Hagedorn, Nora, and Terenzini 1996). Not surprisingly, students' precollege levels of internal attributions for success were the most powerful predictors of end-of-year measures of the same variable (roughly four times the strength of any other predictor), a finding that underscores the power of enduring attributional beliefs or styles. Nevertheless, a cluster of faculty teaching behaviors also exercised statistically significant influences on students' attributions. Students' perceptions of teachers' organization and preparation wielded the second most powerful source of influence on their internal locus of attribution for their academic successes among the host of precollege, institutional, and experiential (academic and nonacademic) variables examined. Rounding out a quartet of statistically significant faculty teaching behaviors were teachers' perceived instructional skill and clarity, teachers' perceived support, and teachers' perceived use of technology (the single behavior of teachers with a negative influence). Although the contribution such behaviors have made to students' learning has already been confirmed, the influence of the behaviors on students' formation of internal attributions for academic success has been less frequently recognized. What is more remarkable is that faculty's influence is discernible, even after a relatively short period of time (less than one year) (Pascarella et al. 1996). An earlier study reached the notable conclusion that good teaching exercised a beneficial effect on causal attributions, weakening the strength of the negative relationship between external, stable attributions and strivings for achievement (Perry and Magnusson 1989). Thus, "from an instructional perspective, these findings imply that one of the major benefits of good teaching is its capacity to compensate for less effective learning orientations" (p. 171).

Faculty can also capitalize on the power of peers' influence on cultivating healthy causal attributions for academic outcomes among their students. In a series of pioneering studies, at-risk students heard videotapes of upper-class students testifying that their own academic performance had improved as they progressed toward their senior year (Wilson and Linville 1982, 1985). Addressing the stability dimension of the at-risk students, the training was designed to encourage students to ascribe failures more to transient causes than to stable ones. The attributional training resulted in higher test grades for participants than those in a control group. Another study with a similar methodological design and results used videotaped remarks by upper-class students that were reinforced by a professor (VanOverwalle, Segebarth, and Gold-chstein 1989). Apparently, students who heard the testimonies of their peers gained confidence that their own academic problems were not insurmountable or a reflection of insufficient ability. More recently, the self-limiting attributional beliefs of high-ability females were reshaped to more positive ones by attributional retraining techniques, and, subsequently, the group exposed to the retraining program achieved greater success on the final examination than a control group (Heller and Ziegler 1996). Unfortunately, not all attempts at attributional retraining have achieved such positive results, and the permanence of changed attributions is unclear.

On the reverse side of the coin, however, some faculty members' practices in giving feedback on performance can foster low-ability ascriptions for performance outcomes, despite their good intent. The practices include excessive praise for a student's performance (particularly on a task that was not overly challenging), unsolicited offers of help, and expressions of sympathy for poor performance, particularly in traditional classrooms emphasizing social comparisons (Graham 1990).

Promoting Adaptive Attributions
For Success and Failure

Causal attributions are but one of a complex set of factors that influence students' motivation for learning and their subsequent achievement. Despite the fact that other factors may have a more direct influence on achievement outcomes, adaptive causal attributions for academic success and failure help create a "can-do" mind-set critical for meeting academic challenges that students are likely to meet as they progress through the educational system. The challenges of college-level work, in particular, may be best met when students give credit to, and capitalize on, both ability and effort for their successes. Students can also develop greater resiliency to failure by attributing failure to factors that can be changed, such as by increased effort or more effective study. In short, adaptive attributional patterns contribute to a healthy psychological profile for students. Faculty, through their classroom behaviors and verbal communication with students, are in a key position to foster adaptive ascriptions for academic outcomes and reshape others so that they are more conducive to further learning and achievement.

Conclusion

College students' attributions, or explanations for academic success or failure, can influence their efforts to succeed in college. Faculty and others may be able to work with college students to promote positive attributions for failures and successes.

Bob is an academic adviser for his college's undeclared majors. One of his advisees is Raymond, who was put on academic probation after his first semester and who, approaching the end of his first year of college, knows that he will likely not fulfill the requirements of his academic contract. Looking at Raymond's records, Bob sees a 1.61 semester average for the fall, with grades ranging from a B in American Cultures to an F in Introductory Economics. Raymond is reasonably sure that he will fail the economics course again this semester and be dismissed from college.

Because the hectic period of fall registration has passed, Bob has a little more time than usual and chats with Raymond about his future plans. Raymond was a high school swimmer and had decided that he wanted to be a high school science teacher and swimming coach. Now, with his mediocre grades in science and mathematics and his trouble with his grade point average, he is at a loss.

Bob decides to take a different approach with Raymond, who is registered for 16 credits for the fall, including Finite Mathematics, Chemistry, Economics 2, Psychology, and Introduction to Education. He processes an override of Raymond's automatic dismissal and then, with Raymond, puts together a "success plan." Beginning in the fall semester, Raymond will enroll for a maximum of four courses per semester and meet with Bob every other week. Bob also arranges for Raymond to work with a local high school swimming coach four afternoons a week and to receive work/study credit for his experience. Raymond also enrolls in College Learning Skills; he will keep Introduction to Education and the next course in his mathematics sequence, Finite Mathematics.

Albert Bandura's work on self-efficacy forms an important basis for consideration of the learning-centered college campus (Bandura 1986, 1993, 1997). This section describes Bandura's developmental work on self-efficacy, reviews research relating it to experiences and achievements of young adults and college students, and suggests links between current approaches to classroom learning, such as group and collaborative class work and academic learning communities, and the development of self-efficacy. The section concludes with suggestions for approaches to learning and research in the context of college that might be useful as we seek to enhance the self-efficacy of college students.

Bandura defines self-efficacy as individuals' "beliefs about their capabilities to produce designated levels of performance that exercise influence over events that affect their lives" (Bandura 1994, p. 71). An individual's perceived self-efficacy is related to motivation in that if an individual believes he or she has the capability to perform a task and that performance will then lead to a positive result, the individual will be motivated to perform (Bandura 1977; Lucas 1990; Sexton and Tuckman 1991).

According to Bandura, motivational processes are generated cognitively (for the most part), based primarily on self-beliefs. Theories of motivation include attribution theory, expectancy-value theory, and goal theory. Beliefs about one's capabilities influence each of these processes. Causal attributions influence perceptions of self-efficacy and are then related to performance (see, e.g., Relich, Debus, and Walker 1986). Beliefs about self-efficacy are involved in a cyclical process in which individuals interpret performance and adjust self-beliefs, which in turn inform and alter subsequent performance (Pajares 1996). Explicit challenging goals enhance and sustain motivation; when people set challenging goals for themselves, a state of disequilibrium is created. This discrepancy is then reduced by accomplishing those goals. These dynamic models describe continual adjustment processes of self-regulation and continuing reevaluation as college students set goals, fail or succeed, readjust, and begin again. Similarly, beliefs about self are slowly modified over time. Beliefs affect behaviors, which affect outcomes, which affect beliefs, and so on.

Self-efficacy and Learning
Bandura's in-depth descriptions of the importance of perceived self-efficacy in learning (1986, 1993, 1994, 1997) are the result of more than 30 years of focused study. Bandura and his colleagues demonstrated that both the self-efficacy beliefs of students and the collective beliefs of teachers (in their instructional efficacy) contributed significantly to levels of academic achievement in school settings (Bandura 1993). Self-efficacy beliefs also produced achievement effects

through motivational processes, either enhancing or decreasing motivation. Self-efficacy influences academic achievement through several mechanisms; it affects an individual's thoughts about, emotional approach to, selection of, and persistence at a task (see Bandura 1993).

Raymond, the student in the case study, has begun to question his self-efficacy in domains where he was previously successful, science and mathematics. If his self-efficacy erodes sufficiently, he is likely to think negative thoughts during performance, react emotionally to expectations for the classes, and avoid or give short shrift to his academic tasks. Bandura claims that no mechanism of personal agency is "more central or pervasive than people's [self-efficacy] beliefs" (Bandura 1993, p. 118). Self-efficacy beliefs influence an individual's feelings, thinking, motivations, and behaviors.

Self-efficacy beliefs influence students' emotions, which, in turn, can influence students' academic performance. Students' beliefs in their own capabilities affect the amount of stress and depression they experience in difficult academic or social situations. For example, a student with minimal coping efficacy may have disturbing thought patterns, leading to test anxiety, which interferes with the student's ability to perform. Subsequent shame over a low grade can exacerbate the anxiety for the next test; on the other hand, pride in a positive achievement can begin to alleviate the anxiety.

Self-efficacy beliefs shape students' lives through their influence on selection of activities, environments, and careers. Self-efficacy also contributes to the type of social reality students construct for themselves through processes of selection. Choices of educational opportunities and social networks are also influenced by students' perceived self-efficacy. In the case study, Raymond begins to question his academic choices, made based on years of success and positive experiences, because of academic difficulties in his first semester in college. Focusing specifically on the transition from adolescence to adulthood, Bandura (1997) describes the particular importance of structured transitions, such as those provided within the context of colleges and universities.

Self-efficacy is highly domain specific (Pressley and McCormick 1995). Thus, high self-efficacy in one domain is not necessarily consistent with the level of self-efficacy in another. For example, a college student might have high self-efficacy with respect to math and science but low self-efficacy with regard to writing or leadership skills. These beliefs about personal efficacy play a key role in a student's choice of career and major. They can be restrictive, for example, when a college student with a low sense of efficacy in mathematics chooses a major because it does not have a mathematics requirement. Self-efficacy beliefs can likewise be enabling for a student who has positive beliefs about his or her own ability to learn difficult material (Bandura 1997).

Students who have a low sense of efficacy in a given domain will shy away from a difficult task, whereas students with a positive sense of self-efficacy are more likely to take risks and attempt challenging tasks. As students move through college and into adulthood, their sense of self-efficacy is likely to crystallize. Challenging tasks that are met successfully will likely increase self-efficacy in ways that promote future attempts at challenging tasks. Conversely, tasks that are too challenging can erode an individual's sense of efficacy and thwart ambition.

Within a learning-centered classroom, structured learning contexts can allow students to engage successfully in activities that capitalize on self-efficacy.

Beliefs about self-efficacy are formed using information from a variety of sources. For the college student, prior conceptions of ability (often based on experiences in previous educational settings), social comparisons (comparative evaluations within classes, living environments, and cocurricular contexts), framing of feedback (the social evaluation of achieved progress or shortfalls), and perceived controllability (locus of control) all combine for the development of self-efficacy. Therefore, building a sense of self-efficacy that promotes learning for college students involves constructing learning environments that (1) construe ability as an acquirable skill, (2) deemphasize competitive social comparisons and highlight self-comparison of progress and personal accomplishment, and (3) reinforce the individual student's ability to exercise some control over the learning environment. A learning-centered classroom can do all of them for its students.

Four kinds of situations can positively influence the development of students' beliefs about efficacy: mastery experiences, vicarious experiences, social persuasion, and somatic and emotional states (Bandura 1994). Within a learning-centered classroom, structured learning contexts can allow students to engage successfully in activities that capitalize on these four main sources of influence on self-efficacy. Self-efficacy can be positively influenced through activities that provide opportunities to experience mastery, watch others like themselves succeed and thus experience success vicariously, and be persuaded by their peers to participate in challenging activities. These learning contexts will assist students in developing positive, less stressful reactions to challenges.

In the case study presented earlier, the adviser works with Raymond to structure a semester that will provide Raymond with an experience that could lead to mastery as well as social persuasion (his coaching of a high school swimming team). Additionally, he structures Raymond's course load so that Raymond will be able to devote more time to his traditionally strong subject, mathematics. Finally, he enrolls Raymond in a course to ensure that his study behaviors match his goals.

Research on College Students
In the last decade, Bandura and others extended research on self-efficacy from precollege to college student populations. That literature can be roughly divided into work relating self-efficacy to academic achievement (Hackett 1985; Hackett, Betz, Casas, and Rocha-Singh 1992; Lent, Lopez, and Bieschle 1993; Lucas 1990; Sexton and Tuckman 1991; Solberg, O'Brien, Villareal, Kennel, and Davis 1993; Wilhite 1990; Zimmerman and Bandura 1994) and work examining career-related self-efficacy (Bergeron and Romano 1994; Brooks, Cornelius, Greenfield, and Joseph 1995; Croteau and Slaney 1994; Luzzo 1993, 1994, 1995; Luzzo and Ward 1995; Niles and Sowa 1992; S.L. Peterson 1993; Rooney and Osipow 1992; Scheye and Gilroy 1994; Stickel and Bonett 1991). The following explanation briefly summarizes studies of self-efficacy related to career choice and satisfaction and then focuses on studies directly related to self-efficacy and academic achievement.

Extensive work has validated measures of career self-efficacy (Luzzo 1993, 1994, 1995; Luzzo and Ward 1995; Rooney and Osipow 1992). In general, career self-efficacy has been examined as an outcome variable in correlation studies of college students (Bergeron and Romano 1994; Brooks et al. 1995; Croteau and Slaney 1994; Niles and Sowa 1992; Scheye and Gilroy 1994; Stickel and Bonett 1991). An examination of the effects of measures of self-efficacy on behaviors found that, for male college students, self-efficacy played an important role in the consideration of careers involving math and science (Post, Stewart, and Smith 1991). Males and females differed in their perceived self-efficacy in the use of computers (Busch 1995), and measures of self-efficacy with computers were increased following classroom instruction and hands-on experience (J. Smith 1994).

In examinations of a national sample of students followed from senior year of high school into college, measures of self-efficacy were found to relate significantly to political activism (Sherkat and Blocker 1993, 1994). An examination of persistence among college students found that career self-efficacy was significantly related to academic as well as social integration in the college environment (S.L. Peterson 1993).

Self-efficacy and the College Classroom

College students' self-efficacy has been the subject of a small but growing body of literature that includes both discursive speculation and empirical study. (See Pajares 1996 for an extensive review of self-efficacy related to academic achievement at all levels of education.) Several authors in addition to Bandura have described the importance of self-efficacy for college students (see Forsyth and McMillan 1991; Howard-Hamilton 1993; Lucas 1990; McMillan and Forsyth 1991), including the importance of African-American female athletes' beliefs about themselves as scholars as well as the collective beliefs of the athletes themselves in influencing academic performance, and possible interventions for improving students' perceptions of self-efficacy (Howard-Hamilton 1993).

Various measures of self-efficacy have consistently demonstrated positive relationships to global measures of academic success (Hackett 1985; Hackett et al. 1992; Lindner and Harris 1992; Sexton and Tuckman 1991; Solberg et al. 1993; Zimmerman and Bandura 1994). For example, a study of the academic performance of 200 students enrolled in an engineering school found that measures of self-efficacy for completing specific academic milestones were strong and significant predictors of grade point average (Hackett et al. 1992).

In one study, some differences in student teachers' beliefs about teaching and personal efficacy were related to differences in some measures that could affect teachers' future success (Woolfolk and Hoy 1990). Additionally, interviews of some women enrolled in doctoral work in mathematics who later transferred out of their doctoral programs found that the women initially chose mathematics because a mentor (usually a parent or a teacher) had convinced them that they had unique ability. At the graduate level, however, most faced skepticism from faculty and fellow students about their seriousness and ability to perform mathematics at that level, gradually eroding their own sense of efficacy in their graduate work as well as their visions of themselves as mathematicians (Stage and Maple 1996).

Some researchers have examined relationships between students' self-beliefs and college students' behaviors (Sexton and Tuckman 1991; Simmons 1996). Simmons (1996) examined the effects of college students' beliefs and attitudes on their approaches to learning and their use of study and learning strategies. Students in the study included both low achievers who had fallen below the institutional minimum required to continue and students in good academic standing. All participants were within one standard deviation of the group mean on measures of precollege achievement (high school percentile rank and SAT scores). Students with a strong sense of academic self-efficacy were more likely to pursue learning goals that emphasized mastery of a subject rather than protection of self-image. They were also more likely to use executive processing, cognitive processing, and environmental control, key processes in students' regulation of their own learning. Students who were more confident of their academic competence were also more certain of their academic majors than those with lower levels of self-efficacy.

In a study that separated beliefs into ability to perform as well as belief that performance would result in a positive outcome, self-efficacy was a strong predictor of performance (Sexton and Tuckman 1991). An ethnographic study of college students with learning disabilities found that students' descriptions about their abilities to succeed were important to them in explaining their success in college (Stage and Milne 1996).

A few studies have examined relationships between measures of students' perceptions of self-efficacy for specific subject matter and performance in a specific task or course (Horn, Bruning, Schraw, Curry, and Katkanant 1993; Lent, Lopez, and Bieschle 1993; Mone, Baker, and Jeffries 1995; Nicaise and Gettinger 1995; Stage and Kloosterman 1991, 1995; Wilhite 1990). One study, for example, found that in a college psychology course, a measure of mathematics self-efficacy and course expectations added significantly to the explanation of mathematical interests, course intentions, and grade in the course over and above variance explained through gender and ability in mathematics (Lent, Lopez, and Bieschle 1993). Others have found measures of self-efficacy to be related to performance in business courses (Mone, Baker, and Jeffries 1995), human development and psychology courses (Horn et al. 1993; Wilhite 1990), and performance on reading comprehension measures (Nicaise and Gettinger 1995).

Finally, self-efficacy has been found to be valid across gender and ethnic subgroups (Hackett et al. 1992; Solberg et al. 1993). For example, Euro-American status as opposed to Mexican-American status was found to predict higher levels of both occupational and academic self-efficacy (Hackett et al. 1992). A study of students in remedial mathematics classes found no significant gender differences in students' sense of efficacy regarding ability to complete difficult mathematics problems and beliefs about the proper approach to solving problems (Stage and Kloosterman 1995). Those beliefs, however, predicted the final grade in the course for women, even after controlling for previous mathematics courses taken and incoming ability.

Although the groundwork has been laid, only a few studies (e.g., Nicaise and Gettinger 1995) have attempted to modify students' sense of self-efficacy to enhance academic performance. Clearly, more work is needed.

Implications for Learning

The three characteristics of learning environments conducive to the development of self-efficacy bear repeating here. When faculty (1) construe ability as an acquirable skill, (2) deemphasize competitive social comparisons and highlight self-comparison of progress and personal accomplishment, and (3) reinforce an individual student's ability to exercise some control over the learning environment, enhanced self-efficacy is likely to occur.

While much that occurs within the context of college courses bolsters a sense of self-efficacy for many students, sometimes that bolstering can be at the expense of other students in the class. We hear periodically of a faculty member or even an academic department that is proud of the fact that a relatively small proportion of students succeed in their coursework. Perhaps they view their role in the university merely as a sorting mechanism rather than as one of helping students develop skills and abilities. We could argue that these faculty serve primarily to erode students' sense of self-efficacy and to divert them from their learning goals, surely counterproductive to their college's mission.

Similarly, posting grades in rank order and using similar percentile ratings of students can serve to undermine the achievements of students who are only beginning to make gains in their skills and abilities at college. Reviewing responses to examinations in class and allowing students with relatively low grades to present their correct answers can serve to promote students' beliefs in their self-efficacy.

The use of collaborative learning, group work, and academic learning communities can promote students' self-efficacy in many ways. Students can see the achievements of others whom they perceive as similar to themselves, observe behaviors modeled by other group members who may have better study skills, and feel social pressure to spend more quality time on assignments for the benefit of the group. These and similar experiences can enhance a student's sense of efficacy and lead to greater motivation to perform academic tasks.

Understanding self-efficacy can help us work with a student like Raymond who is not excelling in the classroom. Raymond's adviser, Bob, recognizes that Raymond has begun to doubt his choice of career. His beliefs about his ability to perform in his chosen area, science, are beginning to erode. Bob encourages Raymond to take a lighter course load, take a course in the development of learning skills, and engage in a limited way in activities and experiences congruent with past successes. Bob hopes that by developing learning skills, experiencing some successes, and being reminded of his reasons for entering college, Raymond will see his goals as achievable.

Raymond, as a swimmer in high school, earned internship credits for managing the swimming team. Similarly, a business major might work as an intern 10 hours a week with a city program for start-up businesses, and a natural resource major might work with physical plant operations on campus. While typically only a limited number of credits might be earned in this manner, if they are placed at a critical juncture in the curriculum, students could gain reinforcement for expansion of their already strong skills, acquire knowledge to develop their self-efficacy, and build motivation to work toward academic goals. At the same time, they work on study skills that might enhance their chances of succeeding.

It is hoped that Raymond's classroom experiences can provide a context for adjustment of his beliefs about his self-efficacy. Through the development of capabilities and the positive framing of feedback on achieved progress, a student's beliefs about himself or herself can become increasingly positive. In turn, motivation to perform and, ultimately, actual performance are enhanced. Ideally, with success and feedback that continues to underscore personal capabilities, beliefs about self-efficacy become even more positive. The student's motivation and performance proceed in a continual reciprocal relationship.

Rather than quickly diverting students from lifetime goals and aspirations, part of our role is to help students find contexts in which they can develop their self-efficacy by capitalizing on their diverse talents and ways of learning.

Conclusion
The concept of self-efficacy as it relates to college students is important to us as we design classrooms and experiences that foster students' success and in our efforts to learn more about learning.

SOCIAL CONSTRUCTIVISM AS
A BASIS FOR LEARNING

The students in Professor Chavella Roth's undergraduate sociology class have broken up into small groups to discuss their progress on the "working-poor" assignment. They have spent the past few weeks in class exploring theory and data about poverty, unemployment, and social policy. To further their understanding of the sources of poverty in the United States, the students are taking a concrete look at how a family on a limited income is able to live in a particular city. The students are constructing a budget and work life for their assigned "family." The small group of Lisa, Ming, Josh, and Chhevi discuss their family budget as Professor Roth joins them.

Lisa begins: "I think I found a job for our wage earner!" She shares a classified ad for bussers and food servers at a cafeteria in town that has options for full- and part-time work, flexible schedules, and meal benefits. "It pays above minimum wage, and it might even include some health benefits, although I know we expected minimum-wage employment to be unlikely to provide health insurance or other benefits."

Ming: "That's true, so we probably need to get the specifics because we need to make sure the health insurance extends to dependents. We need the young kids to be covered, plus we still have to calculate the taxes that would be taken out."

Chhevi agrees, noting that "the disposable income will be much less."

Josh: "According to our map, that restaurant is about 15 miles from our apartment."

Chhevi: "Maybe we should look for a new apartment?"

Lisa points out that a two-bedroom apartment is too small for two adults and two children.

Josh replies, "But it is the only thing that would fit our budget, and we decided that they would get a sleeper sofa."

Lisa: "I still think it's too small for a family of four."

Josh and Lisa consult the city map and offer a solution. "She can take a bus, except that we haven't budgeted for a bus ride twice a day. We're going to have to increase the transportation portion of our budget to at least 10 percent," notes Lisa.

Professor Roth, who has been circulating among the groups of students, asks this group if they have had a chance to look into the requirements for eligibility and regulations for Section 8 housing. The group has not, and the professor reminds them to investigate this option for the family.

Ming reports that the Public Utilities Commission offers funds for assistance with energy payments in the winter.

Chhevi asks for clarification on how to apply for the program and then quickly adds, "But I think it is only supposed to be used in an emergency, so we can't really count on it, I guess."

As the class comes to a close, Professor Roth reconvenes the students and reminds them of the upcoming due dates for their group papers and in-class presentations addressing the question, "How has this investigation of the working poor affected your understanding of the sources of poverty in the United States?"

This glimpse into an undergraduate classroom reveals a complex and interactive model of teaching and learning. Professor Roth, a teacher for over nine years, has not always taught this way. At one time, her instructional methods included lecturing, some discussion, and presentations by individual students. Although her style of teaching today still includes lecturing, she now incorporates opportunities for group projects that require students to translate the concepts they have been learning in class into real-world exercises. The students participating in the working-poor exercise contextualize what they have learned about poverty, unemployment, social services, and social policy. By collaborating, challenging each other's ideas, and sharing ownership of the task, students make meaning of course concepts. Clearly, in this classroom, learning is not a passive operation but can be more accurately described as active and purposeful. This section describes how learning within such an environment can be understood from a social constructivist framework.

Theories of cognitive learning that emphasize the active role of learners in building and interpreting their own understanding of reality are considered constructivist (J. Brooks and Brooks 1993; Driscoll 1994; Steffe and Gale 1995). A constructivist view of learning rests on the assumption that knowledge is constructed by learners as they attempt to make sense of their environments (see, e.g., Lave 1988; Piaget 1970; Steffe and Gale 1995; von Glaserfeld 1995). The notion that learners must interpret and transform complex information if they are to understand it is the essence of constructivism. The metaphor of carpentry or architecture can be used to portray constructivism's emphasis on a dynamic process of developing understanding through building, shaping, and configuring meaning (Spivey 1995). The learner actively builds knowledge. Learning is the result of ongoing modifications in our mental frameworks as we attempt to make meaning out of our experiences. As a theory, constructivism is based on the belief that learning is brought about as a process of active, individual construction of knowledge.

This section explores the principles of the emergent constructivist theory of learning, beginning with a presentation of the philosophical and psychological perspectives on knowledge and learning that are the underpinnings of constructivism. It continues with a discussion of the implications of constructivist theories for teaching and learning in the classroom. Given the social nature of classroom learning, the section elaborates on the social constructivists' assertion that learners arrive at what they know mainly through participating in the social practice of the classroom and through course projects and assignments. Finally, it suggests approaches to teaching and learning in the college classroom that reflect the perspectives of social constructivism, and demonstrates the application of social constructivism by discussing the teaching practices of collaborative and problem-based learning.

Constructivist Views of Knowledge and Learning
Constructivist approaches emphasize learners' actively constructing their own knowledge rather than passively receiving information transmitted to them from teachers and textbooks. From a constructivist perspective, knowledge cannot simply be given to students: Students must construct their own meanings. Constructivism is most often associated with the respective psychological and philosophical work of theorists such as Jean Piaget, Jerome Bruner, Ernst von Glaserfeld, and Lev Vygotsky (Fosnot 1996). This work has implications for students' learning and has profound implications for teaching and learning in college.

The metaphor of carpentry or architecture can be used to portray constructivism's emphasis on a dynamic process of developing understanding through building, shaping, and configuring meaning.

Constructivism's emphasis on students' active role in the construction of their own learning is consonant with the popular teaching approach "student-centered learning" (Prawat 1992). This view, which moves the locus of the learning activity away from the teacher and toward the student, has prompted many of the current reforms in education to emphasize classrooms where the teacher helps students discover meaning. In these classrooms, the instructor's role is typically characterized as facilitating students' investigations and stimulating reflection (Cobb 1994b). Like student-centered teaching, constructivist approaches grant more importance to constructing learner-generated solutions through problem solving than to memorizing procedures and using them to derive the correct answers (Slavin 1997). Student-centered approaches are consistent with constructivism in the value placed on the learners' points of view and on the development of meaningful constructions of learning. Although this approach may seem fresh, the best educators have always known and applied the concepts of constructivism, but they have done so informally, without the guidance of an official theory of instruction (von Glaserfeld 1995).

Versions of Constructivism
Views that knowledge is simply transmitted to students and that learning is merely a function of rote memorization and drilling inadequately represent the complexity of learning in classrooms (J. Brooks and Brooks 1993). Recently, constructivist views of learning have emerged as alternatives to the traditional behaviorist approaches in education (Malone and Taylor 1993). Although behaviorism continues to influence many aspects of education, including classroom management and instructional objectives, constructivism represents a significant step beyond behaviorism (J. Brooks and Brooks 1993; Ernest 1995; Prichard and Sawyer 1994; Steffe and Gale 1995). In fact, constructivism is probably the most current theory in the psychology of learning (Fosnot 1996).

At present, the constructivist approach in education represents a collection of similar approaches rather than a single unified theory (Ernest 1995; Phillips 1995; Prawat and Floden 1994). Although the approaches stem from similar views about learning, the word "constructivism" serves as a summary label that conceals myriad complex differences and diverse arguments among its variations. Some of the forms subsumed under the banner include radical constructivism (e.g., von Glaserfeld), social constructionism (e.g., Gergen), sociocultural approaches (e.g., Bruner), and social constructivism (e.g., Vygotsky).

Each constructivist approach has its own perspectives about how to facilitate the construction of knowledge, but all share some common beliefs, suggest related perspectives on learning, and contribute to instructional practice. Although most variants of constructivism emphasize that learning is a process of the active construction of meaning, they differ in the degree to which the learner is viewed as active and in the nature and influence of social interaction in the process of constructing knowledge (Confrey 1995). For example, constructivist theories influenced by Piaget primarily focus on an individual's cognitive processes with little emphasis on the context in which individuals function. Vygotsky's influence expanded the focus to include greater recognition of the social influences through which contexts, knowledge, and meanings in everyday life are interpreted, constructed, and reconstructed (Das Gupta and Richardson 1995; Driscoll 1994). Similar to the approach to learning outlined by Piaget, this approach also emphasizes the role of experience in the construction of knowledge, but Vygotsky's work places greater emphasis on the role that language, dialogue, and shared understanding play in learners' constructions. The current debate in education tends to center on whether a constructivist approach places primacy on the cognizing individual or the sociocultural effects on learning (Fosnot 1996). In fact, because of constructivism's emphasis on each person's construction of knowledge for himself or herself, it has been charged with ignoring the role of social interaction in learning.

Social Constructivism's Views of Knowledge and Learning

Social constructivism is the perspective guiding the movement in education to expand the focus beyond the cognizing individual and to place learning squarely in a dynamic social context (Confrey 1995; Ernest 1995; Prawat and Floden 1994; Vygotsky 1978). Social constructivists propose a distinct model of constructivism in their assertion that knowledge is a social product created through the social processes of discussion and negotiation (Confrey 1995). Learning and thinking are situated in social contexts rather than occurring solely in an individual's mind. Social constructivists stress the social nature of knowledge, maintaining that meaningful social exchanges between individuals are the primary sources of cognitive growth and construction of knowledge. The essence of the shared experience is "a dialectical interplay of many minds, not just one mind" (Goodman 1986, p. 87). A metaphor for social constructivism is "persons in conversation" (Ernest 1995). Given the social nature of learning in the college classroom and the emerging realization of the limitations of theories of learning that deal only with an individual's construction of knowledge (Driver, Asoko, Leach, Mortimer, and Scott 1994; Jaworski 1994; Prawat and Floden 1994), an elaboration of the perspective of social constructivism on knowledge and approach to learning is warranted.

The social constructivist school of thought argues that all knowledge is culturally mediated and is constructed through the process of negotiation within discourse communities (Confrey 1995; Das Gupta and Richardson 1995; Ernest 1995; Marshall 1992). The construction of knowledge works best when knowledge is understood as culturally negotiated and is influenced by historical factors, and when learning occurs in social settings (Driver et al. 1994; Prawat and Floden 1994). Social constructivist thought draws most heavily on the work of Russian scholar Lev Vygotsky (1896–1934), who suggested that individual meaning develops through language and social interaction (see Daniels 1996; Moll 1990; Vygotsky 1978, 1986). Through the use of language and social interchange, individual knowledge can be challenged and new knowledge constructed. Moreover, the emphasis on social negotiation acknowledges that individuals share reality and knowledge and, most important, are "intersubjectively" constructed (Jaworski 1994; Lerman 1996). Intersubjectivity refers to the mutual understanding that is achieved between people in communication (Rogoff 1990). Because social settings, such as classrooms, are sites for the construction of knowledge, intersubjectivity is a function of the time and place and the goals of the activity and the students (Lerman 1996). For example, the undergraduate classroom described at the beginning of this section demonstrates the way intersubjectivity develops through discussion and, ultimately, the creation of a mutual understanding of the task and of the concepts relevant to the project.

Social constructivism involves certain key features (Jaworski 1994):

- Active construction of knowledge based on experience with and previous knowledge of the physical and social worlds;
- An emphasis on the influence of human culture, where individuals construct the rules and conventions of the use of language;
- Recognition of the social construction of knowledge through dialogue;
- Emphasis on the intersubjective construction of knowledge, in that knowledge is socially negotiated between significant others who are able to share meanings and social perspectives of a common *lifeworld*.*

According to Vygotsky, the world is a complicated place to understand because what is known is culturally negotiated; that is, what is known about rules and belief systems, what exists, and what is valued are all socially constructed. Understanding becomes deeper and more complex with the opportunity to witness other minds at work and under the pressure of making sense of the challenges and differing versions of knowledge offered by others. This view confirms the critical role of others, particularly more skilled members of the culture, to facilitate the learner's appropriation of cultural understanding (Driver et al. 1994; Lave 1988).

"Knowledge and understanding are constructed when individuals engage socially in talk and activity about shared problems and tasks" (Driver et al. 1994, p. 7). Learning is conceived of as a dialogic process in which the teacher provides the appropriate experiential evidence and introduction to the conventions of the field to guide students' learning. This dialogic process and guided introduction drive cognitive development. A vivid conceptualization of the significance of social interaction in cognitive development is a proposal to relocate cognition from psychology, where the focus is on the individual, to social anthropology, which is in fact a study of a complex social phenomenon (Lave 1988). This proposal clearly extends Vygotsky's emphasis on the social by asserting that learning is a process of integration into a community of practice. This view suggests, for

Understanding becomes deeper and more complex with the opportunity to witness other minds at work and under the pressure of making sense of the challenges and differing versions of knowledge offered by others.

---

*See Berger and Luckmann 1966 for a discussion of the word "lifeworld."

example, that for students of history and math to learn these subjects, they need more than abstract concepts. They need to be exposed to the use of the domain's "conceptual tools" and to instructors who, acting as practitioners, use these tools to resolve problems within the academic discipline or profession. Learning is a process of "enculturation." The aim of the history or mathematics instructor then is to help students appropriate the culture of the discipline.

Educators employing beliefs of social constructivism are distinguished by their efforts to provide learners with the conditions that promote socially negotiated knowledge. These conditions include:

- Students' active involvement in the social processes of the classroom;
- Emphasis on the critical role of peers, in particular more skilled students, in promoting understanding;
- Enculturation of students into the community of the particular academic discipline or profession;
- Emphasis on the common construction of knowledge that results when students involved in an activity negotiate their individual accounts and arrive at some level of agreement (which could be regarded as intersubjectivity);
- Overt use of the sociocultural context to promote learning;
- Use of relevant situations in which students are called upon to resolve dilemmas; and
- Appreciation of multiple perspectives.

Many of these conditions are depicted in the undergraduate classroom described earlier and are highlighted in the following subsection. It is worth noting, however, that discussion about and research on social constructivism is rooted in K–12 education and is only beginning to appear at the postsecondary level.

Toward a Social Constructivist Model of the College Classroom

Social constructivist approaches have influenced current thinking in a variety of fields and disciplines, in particular, science, mathematics, language, and the humanities. Although constructivist and social constructivist approaches have been debated and successfully applied in K–12 education, less evidence is available that these perspectives have been discussed and infused at the postsecondary level (J. Brooks and

Brooks 1993; Love and Love 1995). A review of the literature on social constructivism in higher education reveals that the approach has been employed as a framework for reconceptualizing the college classroom, emphasizing the importance of active learning and social negotiation (Cobb 1994b); reconceiving interactions between teacher and student, and among students (Cross and Steadman 1996; Dimant and Bearison 1991; Light 1990, 1992); and demonstrating the ideas behind such teaching practices as collaborative and problem-based learning (B. Smith and MacGregor 1992). Researchers and some educators in particular disciplines (for example, composition, science, and mathematics) have focused more extensively than others on exploring constructivism and social constructivism as perspectives of how college students learn.

In part, some of the impetus for the adoption of social constructivist approaches in college classrooms is rooted in the national call to change how and what is taught in college (Chickering and Gamson 1987; Prichard and Sawyer 1994; Wingspread Group 1993). Current modifications include the transition from traditional 50-minute, content-driven lecture classes where passive students are isolated from one another and the instructor to classes where students must talk about what they are learning, relate it to past experiences, apply it to authentic problems, collaborate with their peers, actively construct their own meaning, and incorporate the diverse perspectives of others (Barr and Tagg 1995; Meyers and Jones 1993; Prichard and Sawyer 1994). Social constructivist approaches can be useful as general orienting frameworks within which to address these transformations.

Application of the social constructivist perspective in the college classroom leads to models where teaching and learning are portrayed as social exchanges between teachers and students and among students (Billson and Tiberius 1991; Driscoll 1994; Prawat and Floden 1994). The class, for example, is seen as a group or team engaging in group activities in the college classroom (Billson and Tiberius 1991; Michaelson 1994). Learning is cooperative and teaching facilitates the group's learning rather than being a one-way transmission of knowledge. Social interaction and participation in the social context of the college classroom are important in promoting learning (Bruning 1994).

Other perspectives of the college classroom (see, e.g., Driver et al. 1994 and Jaworski 1994) stress social constructivism's conception of learning as enculturation into the community of a particular academic discipline or profession, asserting that classroom learning must focus on the kinds of social engagements that enable students to participate in the cultural practices of the discipline (Driver et al. 1994). These descriptions emphasize the notion that students in mathematics must acquire the language and concepts of the community of mathematicians (Lerman 1996). The descriptions of learning as initiation into a discipline's ways of knowing indicate the role that faculty play in helping learners mediate knowledge, make personal sense of the ways knowledge is generated, and ultimately become enculturated into a disciplinary community.

Using real problems for students to solve helps them to understand complex conceptual theories (Jaworski 1994; Prawat 1992). The use of authentic tasks, or "situated learning" (J. Brown, Collins, and Duguid 1989), is advocated in a work on collaborative design among engineering students (Gay and Grosz-Ngate 1994), which asserts that collaborative student groups, working on authentic computer-based engineering problems, not only learned the concepts under discussion but also experienced how engineering projects are conducted in the workplace. Situated learning is consonant with social constructivism's focus on the overt use of sociocultural context and relevant situations to promote learning.

Expanding on the idea of situating learning in a sociocultural context is the social constructivist principle of locating learning in the context of reality. Based on her work in mathematics, one author advocates beginning with real problems and then letting students use their existing knowledge of the world coupled with the application of complex conceptual theories and ideas learned in class and through textbooks to solve these problems (Jaworski 1994). The emphasis on a realistic task is evident in the example of the undergraduate sociology class earlier in this section. Professor Roth deliberately uses the social and local context by assigning students an activity, situated in proximal cities, that requires them to go out into the community to find information about such issues as housing regulations and public utilities. In the process of addressing the needs of a specific family in a particular context, the students further their understanding of such concepts as "working poor" and "unemployment." Such concepts are progressively developed through the students' involvement in an assigned activity situated in reality.

The acceptance and incorporation of teaching practices like collaborative and problem-based learning in college classrooms provide evidence of the application of social constructivism in higher education. Because of its emphasis on the positive interdependence among students and the communal construction of knowledge in groups, collaborative learning expounds on the social and intersubjective construction of knowledge associated with social constructivism (see, e.g., Bruffee 1993; MacGregor 1990; Wren and Harris-Schmidt 1991). Again, the study of students participating in a collaborative engineering design project examines how the students solved design problems by sharing information and coordinating their activities; providing students with an "authentic experience" enables their socialization into a community of practice (Gay and Grosz-Ngate 1994). Problem-based learning approaches highlight social constructivism's emphasis on the resolution of dilemmas and the construction of knowledge through mediation and negotiation with others (Barrows 1996; Gijselaers 1996).

Through the process of social interchange, something shared by learners can grow in the college classroom. This shared sense of what is known can be considered "common" or "intersubjective" knowledge. The literature regarding the promotion of intersubjectivity among students and between the teacher and students suggests the need for a variety of conditions in the college classroom. One condition relates to the interaction between students and teacher. Faculty members should strive to share authority and reduce the subjective differences between teacher and students, participate in group discussions and projects with the students, prompt students, encourage the free exchange of ideas without one or two people dominating the conversation, encourage positive group dynamics, teach students how to share tasks, and attend to any problems that may crop up in the group (Jaworski 1994; Lerman 1996). In essence, a new conception of the interaction between teacher and students and among students needs to be created.

The interaction between instructor and students in the social constructivist classroom

Vygotsky emphasized the role of the teacher in the educative process. His concept of "the zone of proximal development" provides some measure of the learner's development as related to instruction offered. The zone of proximal development is defined as the distance between the learner's current level of independent problem solving and what he or she is able to do with adult guidance (Jaworski 1994). Vygotsky suggested that with appropriate instruction, a learner could potentially reach higher conceptual levels than what might be achieved without instruction.

A conception of the interaction between teacher and students in the science classroom is one where the teacher works to shape the learners' understanding toward culturally accepted knowledge of science (Driver 1995). With the teacher serving as mediator and guide, students are introduced to the concepts, models, and conventions of the scientific community. Because the nature of scientific knowledge is socially constructed, students must be "initiated into scientific ways of knowing" to learn science (Driver et al. 1994, p. 6). In a social constructivist college classroom, the faculty member provides appropriate experiential evidence and introduces the conventions of the field to guide students' learning.

This guided interaction between students and teacher is consistent with the concept of "cognitive apprenticeship" (J. Brown, Collins, and Duguid 1989). Cognitive apprenticeship refers to the process whereby a learner gradually acquires expertise through the process of working closely with an expert who provides a model and gradually socializes the student into the culture of the profession or field (Gardner 1991). In higher education, the apprenticeship model is commonly employed in academic programs such as teacher education, medicine, business, and engineering (see, e.g., Stinson and Miltner 1996). Modifications to the traditional "master-apprentice" relationship, however, have evolved into a model where learning is given structure by understanding the social practices of the discipline or profession (Garrison 1995). This focus on socialization into a community of practice is significant, because it emphasizes the broad social context of learning. Variations on apprenticeships, including internships and experiential education, are also suggested by social constructivism's emphasis on learners' guided introduction to the socially accepted knowledge of the field.

The interaction among students in the social constructivist classroom

The intellectual skills learners acquire are directly related to how they interact with other learners (Moll 1990; Vygotsky

In a social constructivist college classroom, the faculty member provides appropriate experiential evidence and introduces the conventions of the field to guide students' learning.

1978). As learners collaborate, they internalize and transform the assistance they receive from others, connect new ideas to prior knowledge, and eventually use these same means of guidance to direct their future constructions. Social constructivism supports the use of peer learning techniques: Through talking with each other, students more easily discover and construct interpretations of the concepts. For example, the undergraduate sociology class described at the beginning of this section portrays the occurrence of learning through interaction with peers. The four students shared ideas and conceptions of their task, and jointly tried to make sense of the new information they had gathered. Research on college students suggests that the student-student interactions characteristic of peer learning groups support students' gains in achievement (Cross and Steadman 1996).

Supporters of Vygotsky's view stressing the role of the more knowledgeable other in facilitating learning advocate the practice of pairing more competent students with less competent ones to induce learning (Driscoll 1994). This view is in keeping with Vygotsky's description of a learner's zone of proximal development in that the more advanced student can help promote his or her peer's progress to the next level of understanding. For cognitive growth to occur in the interaction among peers, one partner should be "more capable" (Rogoff 1990, p. 148), which is consonant with the notion of "scaffolding" in which the instructor or more advanced peer functions as a support extending the learner's range as he or she constructs knowledge. This approach was supported in a study indicating that when college students were paired with a more advanced peer, both students benefited (Dimant and Bearison 1991). The "mismatched" pairs used more planning strategies, reasoned out loud, and interacted more frequently than the students paired with a peer at a similar level. Numerous other researchers, however, indicate that both heterogeneous and homogeneous groups of students have mixed effects on students' learning (see, e.g., Blumenfeld, Marx, Soloway, and Krajcik 1996; Cooper 1995; Lou, Abrami, Spence, Poulsen, Chambers, and d'Apollonia 1996; McNeill and Payne 1996; Slavin 1995).

Collaborative Learning and Problem-Based Learning
Current teaching practices that foster social interaction and the co-construction of knowledge include collaborative learn-

ing and problem-based learning. Although these approaches were not derived from social constructivism or are not new to higher education, they highlight the ways that principles of social constructivism can be applied to the college classroom. The practices outlined in the following paragraphs are complementary in that problem-based instruction usually takes place in collaborative learning situations.

The widespread adoption of collaborative learning, a process in which the ongoing exchange among students serves a central educational function (Bruffee 1993), offers one piece of pedagogical evidence that social constructivism can be successfully embraced by education. Collaborative learning promotes the communal construction of interpretation and understanding through a process of critical engagement with and the incorporation of the views of others. The undergraduate classroom described at the beginning of this section offers a glimpse of collaborative learning. Traces of the influence of the collaborative format on these students' ability to link what is known to them to what is becoming known can be seen during their discussion about an opportunity for employment for the family wage earner in their project. Through group discussion, the students gathered what is known, took in and considered the new information and ideas shared by others (such as the information about health benefits and the new concern about transportation), and then constructed a new understanding about important factors to consider in their decision about employment. In this case, the experience of hearing others' ideas and receiving immediate feedback on proposed solutions stimulated group members' understanding. A successful collaborative project includes positive interdependence among the students, a product to which everyone contributes, and a sense of commitment and responsibility to the group's preparation, process, and product (MacGregor 1990). Collaborative learning elaborates on social constructivism's emphasis on social interaction and the communal construction of learning. Moreover, the intersubjectivity essential to effective collaborative learning implies a shared sense of power and authority, where inequality among students resides only in their respective understandings.

In a break from traditional medical education, with its focus on memorization, fragmentation, and lack of attention to the teaching of problem solving, medical schools in the mid-1970s began adopting problem-based curricula (Barrows

1996). Practical problem solving became recognized as a crucial way to prepare physicians for the demands of professional practice. In problem-based learning, problems serve as the springboard for learning. Problems range from a single phenomenon in need of an explanation to a complex simulation or a real situation. Instruction in problem-based learning typically begins by introducing students to disciplinary knowledge and then assigning a problem to promote the use of that knowledge. Working in small groups with the assistance of a faculty tutor, students generate questions, exchange ideas, and construct meaning. The faculty tutor coaches the group by providing support to facilitate students' productive interaction, by asking questions and monitoring the problem solving, and by helping students identify knowledge needed to resolve the problem (Gijselaers 1996; Svinicki, Hagen, and Meyer 1996). Following its success in medical schools, problem-based learning caught on in other areas of education and professional schools and in other college courses.

Problem-based learning is grounded in constructivist theories of learning (Gijselaers 1996). Its use of social and contextual factors to influence learning, however—the emphasis on social interaction among students and instructor by expressing ideas, sharing responsibility, and seeking different views on a problem—aligns it more closely with social constructivism. The undergraduate classroom described earlier offers a sense of problem-based learning in that the students are learning about course subject matter by tackling real problems in a social context. In attempting to understand the problem, the students must work together, discussing, comparing, reviewing, and debating what they have learned. The goal is to stimulate students to use their knowledge to solve meaningful, real-world problems.

Problem-based learning has captured the interest of faculty members in a variety of courses and fields, including undergraduate science classes, master's-level business courses, leadership education, and engineering classes (Wilkerson and Gijselaers 1996). Problem-based learning extends the use of technology and multimedia as the basis for solving problems, and provides new ways for involving students in large lecture classes (Allen, Duch, and Groh 1996). Problem-based learning is valued because it actively involves students in constructing knowledge and developing skills in using that knowledge for analyzing problems and negotiating in a collaborative learning environment (Margetson 1994; Wilkerson and Gijselaers 1996). And problem-based learning encourages students to actively participate and question in class.

Dilemmas Associated with Social Constructivism
The transition to social constructivist instructional practices, such as collaborative learning and problem-based learning, can be difficult for both teachers and students. The role of the faculty member differs in social constructivist approaches from that of the traditional classroom. The faculty member spends far less time in front of the class lecturing and transferring information to students. Rather, the role becomes one of facilitator and coach. Because most students have progressed through a typical educational system where knowledge is taught through lectures, and have relied on memorization and regurgitation on multiple-choice or essay examinations to demonstrate their learning, it is not surprising that students feel threatened or express frustration when they encounter social constructivist approaches. Statements from students, such as "How are we supposed to do this?" and "If you would only tell us what you want, we'll do it," can be expected. The new style can be particularly difficult for students who have performed well in structured learning environments. Moreover, the developmental levels of first- and second-year college students may limit their receptivity to instructional practices where they are expected to learn from their peers rather than from the teacher.

Education under the rubric of social constructivism, which actively considers the cultural and social context of cognitive development, raises important questions about how race and gender mediate learning. For example, given social constructivism's active consideration of students' previous experiences in relation to how they construct meaning, it is important for faculty to recognize students' varied backgrounds and to appreciate different ways of knowing. Social constructivism supports one of the foundational tenets of multiculturalism through its emphasis on the importance of learners' sharing and valuing each other's perspectives. Critics of social constructivism are quick to point out, however, the approach's lack of attention to notions of power. Because people with power tend to be more active in the construction of knowledge, they exert greater influence in what is constructed (Garrison 1995). Although educators are wise to examine the concept of power in the classroom, at the least social constructivism offers a framework in which to destabilize some of the traditional ways power operates in the classroom, recasting the conventional role of student and instructor. The instructor is characterized as coordinator and facilitator, and students' role in the classroom is enhanced in that they are increasingly involved in shaping and directing learning. These reconceptions can help diffuse authority in the classroom, particularly if the instructor is able to moderate interaction among students to equalize participation and reduce dominance by one or two students.

Conclusions

This section has explored an emerging theory in education, social constructivism. Social constructivists stress the social nature of knowledge, maintaining that meaningful social exchanges between students and faculty are the primary sources of learning. By exploring the kinds of instructional practices that would be favored by social constructivism, including collaborative learning and problem-based learning, a framework is offered for understanding and conceiving of new ways to facilitate active learning in the college classroom.

Twenty-eight Chicano, African-American, and white working-class students arrive at an urban community college the first day of their English literature class expecting to once again experience a curriculum distant from their own knowledge gained on the streets. The students enter the classroom and file into rows of seats that face the front of the room. The classroom is quiet and intellectual curiosity absent as students open their notebooks in preparation for taking copious notes on Professor Denton's lecture.

Six weeks later, the students enter the same classroom and immediately gather in small groups. The room is filled with noise and movement, and it is difficult to locate Professor Denton amid the activity. In one of the small groups, four Chicanas are engaged in a lively dialogue about *Over the Ivy Walls: The Educational Mobility of Low-Income Chicanos* (Gandara 1995).

Jessica: This book talks about what "went right." It talks about Chicano lawyers and doctors and. . . .

Maria: There aren't hundreds of Chicano lawyers in my neighborhood! I don't know where the Chicanos Gandara talks about live. I can hardly scrape up the loans for community college, but I'm sure the government will keep pouring out the funds for medical school.

Yvonne: Yeah, and the money for child care for Jose while you study and go to school.

[Professor Denton sits down in this group, but the discussion continues uninterrupted and the students do not focus on the new member of the group.]

Maria: And so what does this mean anyway? That if I didn't have the right parents, or happen into a white school, or—that it's my fault if I don't succeed? Most of my friends are working fast food, or in the factories, or taking care of their kids. Does this mean it's their fault for not being as "successful" as these Chicanos?

Ana: Can we focus back on Gandara? It doesn't really matter if we are leading a different life. Yeah, you're right, I've got kids to feed and bills to pay and a job to go to. So can we finish this assignment so we can get on with it?

The dialogue continues as the professor encourages students to identify and name the multiple issues that have been raised. Themes emerge that are based in the reality of the students' lives: "blaming the victim" for lack of educational attainment, biculturalism, gender differences among Chicanos, teenage pregnancy and child care, poverty in the Chicano community, and defining "success." As the students talk with each other and read, they learn that many aspects of these problems are rooted in the social realm, and they increasingly see how their personal stories around these themes fit into the larger socioeconomic, cultural, and political context. The professor guides the students in their search for other readings that bridge the distance between students' lives and society.

Paulo Freire, a Brazilian educator world renowned for his pedagogic theories, offers insights into learning theory that can inform our practice. Freire's teachings are most often associated with education in nonindustrialized countries, where they have been instrumental in many of the literacy campaigns conducted during recent decades in Latin America and Africa. Educators are increasingly recognizing the applicability of Freire's ideas to educational practices in industrialized countries, however, and applying Freire's perspectives on learning to both formal and informal education in the United States (Best 1990; Faltis 1990). Paulo Freire believes that all persons can discover their ability to learn and acquire knowledge. Central to his beliefs about learning, summarized in *Pedagogy of the Oppressed* (1970b), are:

• Democratic dialogue in the classroom
• A curriculum situated in the learner's reality
• Participatory teaching formats
• Student-centered learning.

This section describes central concepts of Freire's philosophies and methodologies regarding learning, using practical examples that relate to the case study. It begins with a brief discussion about the nature of Freirian pedagogy, addressing three fundamental components of Freire's theories of learning: views regarding learning and the acquisition of knowledge, the purpose of education, and relationships between teacher and students. These concepts form a student-centered framework within which critical and problem-posing pedagogy can occur in the academic classroom. The section concludes with a review of the literature on the applications of Freire's theory to learning in the college classroom.

The case study illuminates two very different learning environments within the academic classroom—a more traditional "factory model" classroom on the first day and an active, engaged, democratic environment in the traditional classroom setting six weeks later. How did the transition between these two academic learning environments take place? Educators observing the classroom might note aspects of collaborative learning techniques, problem-based curricula, and student-centered learning. But the transition did not result simply from carefully applied methods or the latest teaching practices. Using Freirian pedagogy as a theoretical foundation requires not just new methods applied to the college classroom, but also a different way of viewing knowledge, the purpose of education, and relationships between teachers and students.

More Than a Teaching Method
Often educators say they are using Freirian teaching methods in the classroom. Freire's ideas, however, are not simply a teaching method (Giroux 1993). "Nothing can be [farther] from Freire's intention than to conflate his use of the term pedagogy with the traditional notion of teaching. For he means to offer a system in which the locus of the learning process is shifted from the teacher to the student" (Aronowitz 1993, p. 8). Rather, Freirian pedagogy necessitates a shift toward student-centered learning, including a democratic and transformative relationship between students and teacher, students and learning, and students and society. Further, Freirian pedagogy requires challenging traditional beliefs about what constitutes knowledge and what it means to know.

Freirian pedagogy requires instructors to examine their views regarding learning, the acquisition of knowledge, and the purpose of education; transform relationships between teachers and students; and reconsider curricular content (Freire 1970b). Applying Freirian "methods" without these concomitant changes co-opts these methods and results in ends similar to those of traditional teaching methods. For example, students' beliefs that they have no "legitimate" knowledge to share with others may be reinforced.

Moreover, both content and methods must be considered in developing this critical, liberatory pedagogy. "Emancipatory content presented in a nonliberatory way reduces critical insights to empty words that cannot challenge students' taken-for-granted reality and cannot inspire commitment to radical change" (Frankenstein 1983, p. 318). Likewise, although humanistic methods without critical content may make students "feel good," the methods alone cannot help students become subjects capable of using critical knowledge to transform the world (Frankenstein 1983).

Learning and the Acquisition of Knowledge
The banking concept of learning
On the first day of class, the students in the case study file into the rows of chairs expecting to passively take notes from Professor Denton. These students, like most of those entering institutions of higher education, come from elementary and secondary education systems where students often participate little in the learning process (Love and Love 1995). Unfortunately, higher education often continues this tradition of nonparticipation in which the transmission of knowledge is unidirectional through practices such as whole-group instruction, instructor-dominated lectures, students sitting passively in the classroom with an instructor viewed as the source of knowledge, and a focus on the development of basic skills. This dominant model of learning, or the "banking theory" of education (Freire 1970b), views students as empty receptacles into which teachers deposit knowledge.

The Freirian concept of learning
This prevalent theory of education is an authoritarian form of education that limits students' creative powers for critical thought, resulting in students who are passive, dependent, alienated, and hopeless as they accept the "received view" fatalistically as "known reality" (Freire 1970b). In addition, the traditional banking concept of education assumes that students' cognitive structures are such that the simple exposure to well-formulated knowledge is effective. Curricula are subsequently broken down into specialized tasks to be taught individually and sequentially (for example, drill students in grammar to sharpen their writing skills). This behavioristic approach to education decontextualizes knowledge (Giroux 1993).

In contrast to the banking concept of education, Freire (1970b) views learning as socially constructed, situated within a sociohistorical context, nonpositivistic, and an ac-

This dominant model of learning, or the "banking theory" of education views students as empty receptacles into which teachers deposit knowledge.

tive process. The case study at the beginning of this section illustrates a Freirian view of learning and the acquisition of knowledge. A nonpositivistic approach to knowledge is evident as students socially construct knowledge in the classroom through dialogue, interaction, critical reflection, and action. Within the framework of Freirian pedagogy, learning is viewed as an active process that involves transformation; "to learn is to re-create the way we see ourselves, our education, and our society" (Shor 1993, p. 26). In the case study, the professor and the students engage in an active process of creating and knowing. Students do not assume that the professor will "transmit" a given body of knowledge but take an active role in learning by questioning "known reality" and transforming their self-views and lives. Moreover, learning is not decontextualized but remains situated in the students' reality. For example, instead of honing writing skills through drills, students learn to examine critically, critique, and write while examining problems relevant to their lives. Students connect readings to their personal stories and through critical dialogue fit these stories within a larger sociohistorical context.

Conscientization

At the core of Freire's educational philosophy (1970b) is his theory of *conscientization*. Conscientization refers to the process through which students achieve a deepening awareness of the sociocultural reality that shapes their lives and of their capacity to transform that reality through action upon it (Freire 1970a, 1970b). Learning begins with the present level of consciousness as manifested in students' language, self-concept, world view, and present living conditions. Conscientization has four levels:

1. *Intransitive consciousness:* People are preoccupied with their most elementary needs and have little or no comprehension of their sociocultural situations.
2. *Semiintransitivity or magical consciousness:* People take the facts of their sociocultural situations as "givens." They are characterized by low self-efficacy and an external locus of control.
3. *Naive, semitransitive consciousness, or popular consciousness:* A serious questioning begins at a primitive level. People begin to sense that they have some control

over their lives, and silence is less characteristic of this level.

4. *Critical consciousness:* People at this level deeply and critically interpret problems, exhibit self-confidence in discussions, and take action as part of their refusal to shirk responsibility. Discourse is dialogical at this level. People who think holistically and critically about their conditions reflect this highest level of thought and action. Critical consciousness is not the result of intellectual effort alone. Rather, critical consciousness results through praxis, or the authentic union of action and reflection.

The case study helps illustrate how college students may be at different levels of conscientization. For example, the dialogue among the four Chicanas appears to show the majority of these students at the level of semiintransitivism or magical consciousness. These women generally view their sociocultural situation as a "given," sensing that they do not have much control over their lives. Intransitive consciousness appears to more accurately describe Ana's present level of consciousness, however: She is preoccupied with her basic needs.

As the dialogue continues throughout the semester, these women's learning processes might bring them through various levels of conscientization. For example, Maria might increasingly engage in a critical questioning of her reality, leading to a deepening awareness of her sociocultural situation that is characteristic of naive (semitransitive) consciousness. Further, as they become more critically conscious of the way society affects their lives and begin to use writing as a means of intervening in their own social environment, these women may exhibit critical consciousness.

Students who reach the level of critical consciousness would not only interpret problems critically but also take action. This action is imperative, given the importance of praxis to critical consciousness. For example, later in the semester Jessica might decide to use a course writing assignment to write a letter to the editor about "blaming the victim," in this case Chicanos, for not attending institutions of higher education. She might bring the letter back to the group to gain feedback and critical insight before submitting it to the newspaper. Or Maria and Yvonne might collaboratively research the root causes of low educational attainment among

Chicanos, engage their classmates in dialogue about this problem to gain critical insights, and ultimately decide to schedule a meeting with the local school board to discuss increasing support for the education of Chicanos. And Ana might establish a chat room on the Internet to discuss race and poverty with others; as she struggles with this issue, she might begin to work with low-income high school youth through a community mentoring project.

Although *Pedagogy of the Oppressed* (Freire 1970b) presents learning as a process of moving from one level of consciousness to another, a later work acknowledges that levels of consciousness often overlap (Freire and Faundez 1989). The nonlinear characteristics of conscientization have been noted in the frequent movement between critical insight and myth evident in students' journals (Frankenstein 1983). Students often maintain strong critical insights in some areas of life while simultaneously engaging in a non-critical approach to knowledge (Frankenstein 1983).

The Purpose of Education

From Freire's perspective (1970b), education's role is to challenge inequality and dominant myths rather than socialize students into the status quo. Learning is directed toward social change and transforming the world, and "true" learning empowers students to challenge oppression in their lives.

Freirian pedagogy is often constructed as being "too political" in that the learning process either reinforces or challenges existing social forces. Freire argues, however, that all forms of education are contextual and political whether or not teachers and students are consciously aware of these processes. Within the discourse of the classroom, for example, politics is evident in the way teachers and students talk to each other, in the questions teachers pose and the themes chosen for study, in the freedom (or lack thereof) students feel in questioning the curriculum, and in the silences that often surround unorthodox questions in traditional classrooms (Shor 1993). Accordingly, Freire emphasizes the importance of examining the nature of the knowledge we teach and our views of the purpose of education.

Teacher-Student Relationships

Learning in the traditional "banking model" classroom often involves characteristics such as one-way transactions and communication, vertical power relationships between educators and learners, and prescriptions or directives for learners to follow (Shor 1993). In academic classrooms, students often enter class (as did the students in the case study) prepared to take copious notes from the professor. Moreover, students often lack confidence in, or perhaps even consciousness of, their ability to contribute to the construction of knowledge.

This teacher-student contradiction inherent in traditional classrooms should be resolved "by reconciling the poles of the contradiction so that both are simultaneously teachers *and* students" (Freire and Faundez 1989, p. 59). In other words, Freire's pedagogy calls for a transformative relationship between students and teacher so that both are co-learners or co-investigators in the learning process. As co-learners, teachers and students share curricular and other classroom-related decisions. The case study illustrates the transformative relationship in several ways:

- The distinction between the instructor and the students is blurred, and the professor cannot easily be located in the classroom.
- Professor Denton joins the dialogue in the small group but does not become the focal point of the discussion.
- Professor Denton does not seek to provide answers for students or to serve as the authority, but rather provides opportunities for students to actively participate in analyzing their reality.
- Students share in decisions about readings and projects for the course.

The transformative relationships do not negate Professor Denton's knowledge and contribution to the learning process. The instructor maintains a role in group dialogue and problem posing, and guides students to other sources of useful information. The instructor's role is redefined as a facilitator of learning, however, rather than as the sole provider of knowledge. Students are seen as important co-contributors who are integral in the construction of knowledge. Further, the transformative relationship also reconstructs professors as co-learners open to learning *from* and *with* their students. Indeed, teachers should be humble so they can grow with the group rather than losing their humility and claiming to direct the group once it is animated and actively engaged (Freire 1971).

The relationship between teacher and students is transformed gradually. For example, in the case study, Professor Denton provides some structure at the beginning to meet students' expectations. Professor Denton also plays a role in helping students to ask questions and become aware of their reality. As students become more comfortable with their roles as co-learners and more readily share personal experiences, they begin to ask each other questions and engage in critical dialogue, enabling the professor to step back from the discussion.

Problem Posing

The problem-posing approach to education (Freire 1981; Freire and Faundez 1989) places students' experiences and cultural and personal strengths at the core of the curriculum and engages students in the critical analysis of problems relevant to their everyday lives. "Problematizing" (Graman 1988) is the identification, recognition, and understanding of the significance of problems in relation to students' lives and the lives of others. Subsequently, once students understand the significance of a problem, they will attack problems and develop ways to improve conditions that give rise to them (Graman 1988).

Freire (1981) distinguishes between problem solving and problem posing in his discussions of the process of problematizing reality. Within a problem-solving framework, solutions are found for the students and imposed on them. Problems are expected to have "correct answers," and students are often presented with solutions rather than encouraged to discuss a range of options and devise strategies together. Although the problems presented in the curriculum are often based in reality (or at least in the reality of middle-class white students), the problem-solving approach still places the responsibility for learning on the teacher and does not foster conditions that allow students to identify and think critically about problems.

In contrast, problem posing places the identification and analysis of troublesome aspects of reality as central to the curriculum. The purpose of problem posing is not to find solutions for students, but to involve students in searching for and creating their own alternatives as a response to think-

The problem-posing approach to education places students' experiences and cultural and personal strengths at the core of the curriculum and engages students in the critical analysis of problems relevant to their everyday lives.

ing critically about reality. The teacher's role in problem posing is to problematize reality for the students so that they come to think critically about previously taken-for-granted aspects of reality. This process involves listening to students' generative themes, encouraging classroom dialogue in which students and teachers can collaborate in demystifying taken-for-granted perceptions, and facilitating action based on critical reflection. These parts of the process are described as three phases of problem-posing methodology: listening, dialogue, and action (Wallerstein 1983).

Listening

Given that Freirian pedagogy grounds academic subjects in students' thoughts and language, instructors need to attend to students' life and language. In the problem-posing process, instructors listen for students' concerns to develop what Freire terms "generative themes"—that is, discussion themes arising from students' daily lives around which consciousness can be raised. In the case study, Professor Denton listens to the students' discussion and helps them to identify the generative themes that arise from their personal reflections about Gandara's book. Acknowledging and naming reality through the identification of generative themes (e.g., blaming the victim for Chicanos' low educational attainments, teenage pregnancy and child care, and biculturalism) is a major step toward the development of the students' critical consciousness. This problem-posing approach contrasts traditional learning that invents its themes, language, and materials from the top down rather than from the bottom up.

Dialogue

Freire's (1970b) conceptions of learning focus on dialogue between learners and educators. The basic format of the class is dialogue around problems posed by both instructors and students, with instructors guiding the process into deeper phases. Class discussions encourage self-reflection and social reflection regarding how we talk about issues, how we know what we know, how we can learn what we need to know, and how the learning process itself is working or not working.

Using the generative themes, the instructor encourages this critical dialogue and helps sustain reflective social interaction. The goal of the dialogue is to "decode" the problem, naming, objectifying, and reflecting on the cultural construction of students' reality and what it means. In decoding reality, students, it is hoped, will come to realize that meaning and reality are not static or fixed but that reality is socially constructed and can be transformed.

Some students may be so submerged in a given reality that they are unable to detach themselves from their reality to treat it as an object of reflection. Instructors might try to break the ensuing silence by facilitating reading and critical reflection on readings. Such practices might help students to gain distance from the concrete immediacies of their everyday lives and to increasingly understand how their lives are shaped by and in turn can shape the world (Freire 1983). For example, the four Chicanas in the case study began by discussing Gandara's book. Through this dialogue about the book, they gained enough distance from their own reality to be able to see and name problems from their lives.

Several educators offer guidelines for decoding a problem and moving the discussion from the concrete to the analytic. For example, five steps in the process could be to (1) name the problem (describe what students see), (2) define the problem(s), (3) elicit similar situations in students' lives, (4) direct students to fit their personal stories into the larger socioeconomic, cultural, or political context, and (5) encourage students to discuss alternatives and solutions (Wallerstein 1983). And the "but why?" discussion technique (Werner 1977) can also help get at cultural, socioeconomic, political, and historical root causes by eliciting deeper or different reasons for a problem situation.

Action

Once students have come to understand the significance of problems through authentic analysis and conversation, the next step is to develop ways to overcome the problems and to improve the conditions that give rise to them (Graman 1988). Learning is related to action on one's total environment (Elias 1974), which happens in this way:

> When dialogue is practiced in the classroom, in a Freirian sense, with focus on individual student concerns, learners are engaged in the process; they assume control for learning, and this control, in turn, generates the authority permitting them to act—to transform

their immediate academic concerns as well as their long-term goals (Best 1990, p. 13).

As mentioned, the union of action and reflection is imperative for critical consciousness. Simply stated, dialogue prompts critical reflection, which in turn prompts action. Both are essential to learning (Wallerstein 1983). Action allows students to learn to see themselves as social and political beings, with rights to challenge political and sociohistorical institutions that shape their reality (Wallerstein 1983). Thus, Freirian pedagogy seeks to empower students to not only take charge of their own learning, but also to intervene in their social environment.

Actions resulting from critical analysis and reflection may vary considerably (for example, Jessica might write a letter to the editor, while Maria and Yvonne might schedule a meeting with the local school board to discuss increasing support for the education of Chicanos). Such actions can be integrated formally into the curriculum as a required class project, although the professor should not predetermine the content and particular action, or actions can be allowed to emerge through students' critical reflections. Service-learning courses offer a specific opportunity for students to engage in the critical reflection and praxis of Freirian pedagogy (Muller and Stage 1998). Service learning also provides an avenue for student affairs professionals to participate more fully in students' learning processes (Muller and Stage 1998).

Applications to the College Classroom in the Literature
Much of the literature on Freirian pedagogy consists of philosophy-based discussions of his theories (see Aronowitz 1993; Giroux 1993; Shor 1993). The applicability of Freire's thought to student affairs has been discussed (Manning 1994), but the literature applying Freire's ideas specifically to academic learning and the college classroom is more limited. The literature that does exist tends to focus on several issues: applications to courses teaching English as a second language (ESL), courses for nonnative English speakers and nontraditional students, and resistance encountered in applying Freire to the college classroom. In addition, Freire's ideologies and methodologies have been discussed as an appropriate theoretical foundation for service-learning courses (Muller and Stage 1998).

ESL, nonnative English speakers, and nontraditional students

Writing and ESL instructors replicate many of Freire's principles in their teaching (Best 1990). Teachers do not impose strategies and styles on developing writers but focus instead on students' authentic language production, enabling them to discover their voice and their text. A proposed alternative approach to Spanish for native speakers (teaching Spanish to college-level bilingual native speakers interested in developing their Spanish abilities) draws heavily on Freire's problem-posing procedure for critical dialogue and Vygotsky's theory of social learning (Faltis 1990). Within this framework, the development of language is framed as a by-product of authentic and purposeful social interaction among students, and between the teacher and students, about topics that matter to students. An application of Freire's conception of problematizing to learning a second language discusses how students build critical thinking skills and the language to express those skills by engaging in problematizing reality (Graman 1988). And several authors have pointed out the appropriateness of Freirian pedagogy for students who are marginalized in our schools (e.g., Best 1990; Freire and Faundez 1989).

Resistance

Two common areas of resistance to Freirian pedagogy are noted in the literature: (1) resistance from instructors and (2) resistance from students. An article on applying Freirian methodologies to two sophomore literature classes at Clemson University describes how the instructors sought to subvert the banking concept of education by simply changing positions—rearranging the structure of the classroom to "change the dance" between students and teachers—but found that teaching and being a student in the banking model are ingrained behaviors that are "stubbornly resilient" (Boerckel and Barnes 1991, p. 5). The teachers realized that "when the going got rough, we could not maintain our position" and responded authoritatively to challenges from students (p. 5). Therefore, teachers need to continually examine their own behavior in the classroom.

A reflective journal about students in an in-service teacher education class also illuminates instructors' resistance to Freire's critical pedagogy (O'Loughlin 1990). Teachers often resist the notion that students can be empowered to take responsibility for constructing their own understanding. Instructors' beliefs are culturally constructed ideological systems (often unconscious) that pervade entire ways of knowing and acting, including explicit philosophies of teaching and learning. Instructors often espouse authoritarian and didactic teaching philosophies and practices because that is how they themselves were taught in secondary and postsecondary classes. Educators' constructions of pedagogy are rarely challenged in academic cultures (Stage 1996); indeed, the university reward system has historically not provided incentives for such attention to pedagogy and teaching (Boyer 1990).

In a discussion of resistance from students, two instructors noted that when they removed the comfortable structure in which students were defined as passive learners, many students were completely at a loss (Boerckel and Barnes 1991). "Their confidence in their abilities to interpret a work of literature and even in their ability to understand a work of literature was nil. It was as if they became de-selfed in the face of adopting a new, active role" (p. 3). Students showed two common reactions: refusing to work, or feeling incapable of working (Boerckel and Barnes 1991). Students who have not had the opportunity to assume responsibility for working in a class may have doubts about their own abilities that lead them to remain passive. Other work describes students' resistance to group work and the many problems often associated with group projects that are intended to be collaborative.

Conclusion

Although Freirian pedagogy is increasingly being applied to learning in the college classroom, much research is still needed. In addition to the research, practitioners need to continue to explore the applications of Freire's ideas to the college classroom and adapt Freirian pedagogy to meet specific contexts and needs. But Freirian ideas or methods should not be followed as rigid models. Instead, we need to reinvent liberating education for our own situations (Shor 1993). "The only way anyone has of applying in their situation any of the propositions I have made is precisely by redoing what I have done, that is, by *not* [emphasis added] following me. In order to follow me it is essential not to follow me!" (Freire and Faundez 1989, p. 30).

OTHER THEORIES: Challenging
Classroom Assumptions

Jim Robertson is a popular anthropology professor who has always enjoyed teaching. He prides himself on his high evaluations, which he says he earns while maintaining high standards. He uses a lecture style in his large classes, interspersed with sports metaphors, personal stories about his travels, and occasional jokes about the indigenous peoples he has studied. During class, Professor Robertson often engages in witty intellectual banter with the few students in his large classes who are up to it; as it turns out, they are the ones who usually earn the small number of A's he gives out.

Last fall, Professor Robertson was surprised when his department chair notified him that students had lodged some complaints about his class. Some thought he showed favoritism to males, specifically white males. Others complained that his comments in class were often inappropriate. A small but significant number of written comments in his teaching evaluations followed a similar vein. After his initial shock and anger, Professor Robertson sought advice from an associate professor and friend known for innovative teaching.

Traditions in U.S. college classrooms are based on European styles and expectations from the 15th and 16th centuries (Stage and Manning 1992). Colleges and universities have lasted over 350 years in the United States and are known for their imperviousness to change (often cited as the reason they are among the oldest of the world's institutions). Those traditions carry over into assumptions and expectations in the classroom that do not always serve the purposes of the late 20th century—to educate a broad spectrum of students (Stage and Manning 1992). Professor Robertson's timeworn techniques for educating, while entertaining and demanding as well as witty, seem not to work for all students in his classes.

This section considers two theories that are particularly useful for challenging assumptions about learning and intelligence: Gardner's theory of multiple intelligences and Kolb's learning styles. The theories are helpful for identifying factors that might inhibit the learning process for college students, and they can provide useful guidance as we develop learning-centered classrooms. Although not typically linked theoretically, they share certain similarities when viewed in terms of educators' expectations for their students. Knowledge of both theories can expand in a positive way our views of the cognitive attributes of college students.

Gardner's theory of multiple intelligences (1983) prompts us to contest traditional evaluations of the cognitive attributes of college students. Research based on this theory challenges us to expand notions of intelligence and to devise ways to capitalize on the assets of all our students, not just those whose intellectual characteristics closely match our own (as well as the dominant style of thinking within our discipline). Discussion centers on descriptions of ways of identifying and developing many kinds of intelligence in the academic context.

Kolb's typology of learning styles (1981) and related research (J. Anderson 1988; Claxton and Murrell 1987; Messick 1970; Russell and Rothschadl 1991) also provide a useful framework for examining the college classroom and the learning that takes place there. Discussion centers on ways of expanding the presentation of material as well as varying instructors' expectations for students' performance.

Assumptions about Intelligence and Learning

Recent criticisms of educators' assumptions about intelligence prompt an examination of assumptions about both intelligence and learning. *Aptitude Revisited* (Drew 1996) points out the shortcomings of our educational system when we allow simplistic measures of aptitude, verbal and quantitative test scores, to shape attitudes about students and their abilities to learn. Such assumptions systematically screen students from majors and careers, and disproportionately affect students who are women, minorities, and from the lower socioeconomic classes. Additionally, they create a public citizenry that views itself as helpless in certain domains, primarily mathematics and science.

It is possible that faulty decisions were made during factor analyses that forced measures of intelligence into one unifying factor despite strong evidence of at least two or more strong factors (Gould 1981; see also Drew 1996 for more complete discussions of this controversy in the foundational development of the measure of intelligence).

In overwhelming numbers of testing situations in this country, given our propensity for rankings, we systematically relegate millions to failure. In any given year, fully half our states, half our school districts, half our schools, half our teachers, and half our students are described as below average and hence failures. Similar language proliferates discussions of college-level learning. Indeed, within the resultant educational systems, some might expend more resources trying to influence rankings than trying to influence learning.

If we truly believe that intelligence is fixed and that college students come to us with abilities that predetermine success, what challenge is there in being an educator, beyond the clerical function of sorting? Additionally, knowing that a student ranks in the top half of a class tells us nothing of his or her ability to perform in a complex workplace situation. Beyond the barbaric notions and demoralizing and discouraging effects of sorting and ranking, Gardner (1983) makes a compelling case for consideration of multiple kinds of intelligence (see the following discussion).

The social and cultural systems within which children develop cannot be ignored in discussions of intelligence and learning (Rogoff 1990). Learning within those vastly different social contexts differentially affects what is learned and ultimately can affect performance on cognitive tests. As college populations become more diverse, overreliance on narrow indicators of intelligence and ability becomes more and more problematic for those who are truly interested in educating. Drew's analysis of science and mathematics education challenges assumptions about traditional indicators or predictors of academic success and attempts to create a consciousness that every student "has the capacity to master mathematics and science and should be taught those subjects" (Drew 1996, p. 2). His arguments could extend approaches to other areas of academic learning as well.

As college populations become more diverse, overreliance on narrow indicators of intelligence and ability becomes more and more problematic for those who are truly interested in educating.

Multiple Intelligences

Gardner's theory of multiple intelligences (1983) and subsequent research based on that theory (Gardner and Hatch 1989; Krechevsky and Gardner 1990) provide impetus for educators to expand notions of intelligence. Rather than simplistic notions of bicategorical verbal and mathematical intelligences, this body of work provides evidence of a multitude of intelligences traditionally ignored or undervalued in formal educational settings.

Gardner defined intelligence as "the capacity to solve problems or to fashion products that are valued in one or more cultural settings" (Gardner and Hatch 1989, p. 5). He developed the categories of intelligence by examining research on abilities in a variety of sources, including special populations such as prodigies, autistic individuals, idiots, savants, and learning-disabled children; forms of intellect valued in different cultures; and neurological changes in cognitive capabilities. Based on this and subsequent research, Gardner found at least seven forms of thinking (the seven intelligences) that individuals exhibit.

The two intelligences traditionally emphasized and valued in American and in other industrialized cultures are *logical-mathematical intelligence* and *linguistic intelligence*. To these two, Gardner added five other intelligences that are traditionally undervalued and not stressed in most formal educational systems. *Musical intelligence* refers to abilities to produce and appreciate rhythm, pitch, and timbre, and the appreciation of the forms of musical expressiveness. An individual with *spatial intelligence* has the capacity to accurately perceive the visual-spatial world, typified by navigators or sculptors. *Bodily-kinesthetic intelligence* is manifested in abilities to control body movements, well-developed fine motor skills, and an adeptness in handling objects skillfully; dancers, sculptors, and athletes exemplify this intelligence. Individuals with *interpersonal intelligence,* such as therapists and personnel directors, have the ability to respond effectively to the temperaments, motivations, and desires of others. *Intrapersonal intelligence* is evident in people with detailed, reflective self-knowledge. Such persons are aware of their own strengths, weaknesses, desires, and intelligences. Often, college students with learning disabilities display a high level of intrapersonal knowledge (Stage and Milne 1996). These seven intelligences are not mutually exclusive categories, nor is there any necessary correlation between any two intelligences.

The challenge for those who work with college students is to find ways to value and enable many types of intelligence among the diverse students who come to our classes. For example, a psychology class project might allow a student with heightened musical intelligence to use various musical styles or examples of individual music as the basis for a discussion of human emotion. In a business class, a student who organizes and leads a group project to a useful product might receive credit beyond those of the other group members. And a faculty member might work with a student with learning disabilities by capitalizing on the student's self-knowledge and allowing the student to use a method of expression or performance that capitalizes on special skills rather than relying on weaker ones.

In these and other ways, we can foster the development of intelligences that are traditionally underemphasized and undervalued in the classroom and make the classroom a more interesting and inclusive experience for faculty as well as students.

Multiple Intelligences and College Students

To date, little research on multiple intelligences has focused on college students other than attempts to validate that various kinds of intelligence do exist. A few studies have examined small parts of the theory and reflected on the theory as part of a larger research project (see, e.g., Kelder 1994; Morrin 1987; Rosnow et al. 1994) or focused on adults, but not particularly on college students (Cromwell 1994). A small but growing body of literature describes approaches to classroom design and curriculum that would be conducive to promoting a wider range of intelligences at the college level (Fogarty and Stoehr 1995; Kelder 1994; King 1994; Koontz 1994; Morrin 1994; Rauch 1994; Rega 1993; Seal 1995; Zevik 1994). Currently, however, much of what we know has been learned in precollege education. Clearly, more research needs to be conducted at the college level.

In the case at the beginning of this section, Professor Robertson has structured his class in a manner that highly values his students' linguistic intelligence. As a conscientious educator, he seeks ways to create a conducive learning environment for all his students and to broaden the kinds of intelligence students may express in his classes. Reflection centering around Gardner's forms of intelligence could prompt him to incorporate a wider variety of possibilities for projects than the traditional research paper. Possibilities for topics for his anthropology students include music, maps, written and artistic artifacts, and the dances of the cultures studied. As a result, class presentations make it more likely that a wider range of students participate actively in Professor Robertson's classes. Consideration of students' learning styles can play a hand in similar curricular transformations.

Learning Styles

The notion of expanding our students' expectations can readily be extended to discussions of learning styles (J.

Anderson 1988; Kolb 1981; Messick 1970; Shade 1992). For example, people use nine dimensions of cognitive style to interpret the world around them (Messick 1970). Differences in focus of attention, approaches to problems, development of conceptual relationships, and information processing tend toward consistent patterns in individuals. These patterns show consistency across time and across diverse tasks (Messick 1970; see also Cross 1976 for a discussion of Messick's descriptions).

Learning styles differ according to ethnicity and cultural background (see J. Anderson 1988 and "Diversity and Learning Styles" on p. 72; Shade 1992). A review of the literature notes that African-American students typically differed from comparison groups and frequently were at a disadvantage when other styles were valued (Shade 1992). For example, some studies found that African-American students performed better than others on tasks involving verbal memory but worse on those involving space conceptualization (Leifer 1972; Lesser, Fifer, and Clark 1965; Stodolsky and Lesser 1967.) Others found cognitive differences in style between middle and lower socioeconomic status African Americans (Orasanu, Lee, and Scribner 1979).

Kolb's theory of learning styles, developed in the 1970s, continues to provide a useful theoretical basis for research and teaching in the college classroom while showing us something unique about our expectations for students' learning (Boyatzis and Kolb 1991; Cavanaugh et al. 1995; Cornwell and Manfredo 1994; Enns 1993; Holley and Jenkins 1993; Katz and Heimann 1991; Krahe 1993; Logan 1990; Rothschadl and Russell 1992; Russell and Rothschadl 1991). Kolb (1976, 1981) used a four-stage learning process to develop a complex typology describing students' learning styles that incorporates experiential learning. The theory capitalizes on students' varying preferences for four stages of learning: concrete experience, reflective observation, abstract conceptualization, and active experimentation. Measuring those preferences, Kolb contrasted two dimensions: (1) concrete experience and abstract conceptualization, and (2) reflective observation and active experimentation. Plotting them along two continua resulted in four quadrants describing individuals' preferred learning styles: convergers, divergers, assimilators, and accommodators. *Convergers* are most comfortable with abstract concepts and active experimentation. They prefer practical applications of ideas, rarely exhibit emotion, and usually have specific interests. *Divergers* are most comfortable with concrete experience and reflective observation, often have a vivid imagination, and are able to view concrete situations from a variety of perspectives. *Assimilators* learn most effectively through abstract conceptualization and reflective observation. They excel in working with theoretical models and inductive reasoning. *Accommodators* learn best in a setting that allows for concrete experience and active experimentation; they prefer doing to thinking. Accommodators rely heavily on information from other people rather than theories, are very adaptable, and solve problems intuitively.

Learning Styles and the College Classroom

Kolb's theory and related research have important implications for approaches to learning. Many researchers have validated the presence of differences in learning styles among college students of both traditional and nontraditional age groups (Cavanaugh et al. 1995; Cornwell and Manfredo 1994; Enns 1993; Garvey et al. 1984; Highhouse and Doverspike 1987; Holley and Jenkins 1993; Holoviak et al. 1990; Hudak and Anderson 1990; Katz and Heimann 1991; Krahe 1993; Kruzich et al. 1986; Logan 1990; Posey 1984; Russell and Rothschadl 1991), although a few have questioned the validity of the scales Kolb describes (see, e.g., Geiger et al. 1992; West 1982).

Researchers have found evidence that learning styles do not differ according to age, gender, prior job experiences, and educational attainment (Cavanaugh et al. 1995), while one review of several studies describes abstract conceptualization and reflective observation as more characteristic of males and concrete experience and active experimentation as more characteristic of females (Enns 1993). Others found that students with a particular major tended to favor one learning style over others (Garvey et al. 1984; Heitmeyer and Thomas 1990; Sadler et al. 1978; Sparks 1990).

Some research suggests that learning styles are related to attitudes toward education. Some studies describe improvements in students' learning after the use of learning styles in planning a class curriculum focusing on students' approaches to and attitudes toward learning (Bodi 1990; Laschinger and Boss 1989). A verification of Kolb's developmental descriptions found that as students moved through the university, they improved their ability to learn through a variety of styles (Lassan 1984). Other researchers found relationships between learning style and performance; that is, test results may be affected by the type of testing format (multiple-choice qualitative, open-ended theory, and open-ended quantitative) (Holley and Jenkins 1993). The results suggest that particular modes of testing could give an advantage to students of particular learning styles.

Not surprisingly, most faculty members tend to be assimilators (Kruzich et al. 1986; Rothschadl and Russell 1992; Sadler et al. 1978; Van-Cleaf and Schkade 1987). Abstract conceptualization and reflective observation, characteristic of assimilators, are assets that have become highly developed for those who must "publish or perish" as well as for those who like to play with ideas. Faculty members' styles of thinking and learning heavily influence classroom assignments and evaluations on a typical college campus. Students who match the instructor's style are apt to feel most comfortable and be most successful in class. Those who do not may have fewer opportunities to use their dominant learning style to advantage.*

Faculty members' styles of thinking and learning heavily influence classroom assignments and evaluations on a typical college campus.

Diversity and Learning Styles

Differences in minority and majority students' learning styles may affect their success in college (J. Anderson 1988). Many majority students (as assimilators) are comfortable with the abstract theory and reflective observation typifying learning in the college classroom. Many minority students, however, learn more easily with concrete examples and practical application, characteristic of divergers. While it is not clear why certain racial/ethnic groups seem to cluster at one end or the other along the continuum of learning styles, it appears that a group's cognitive style is strongly influenced by its cultural history (J. Anderson 1988; Rogoff 1990). Nonwestern peoples (American Indians, Mexican Americans, African Americans, Vietnamese Americans, Puerto Ricans, Chinese Americans,

---

*See Claxton and Murrell 1987 and Rothschadl and Russell 1992 for suggestions for faculty who seek to broaden styles that they require of students in their classrooms; Boyatzis and Kolb 1991, Fitzgibbon 1987, Fry and Kolb 1979, Holoviak et al. 1990, Kruzich et al. 1986, Mark and Menson 1982, Stice 1987, and Svinicki and Dixon 1987 for discussions focusing on specific courses or curricula relative to learning styles; and Posey 1984 for a description of ways that administering a learning styles inventory in a class might be used to help students develop their own strategies for study.

Japanese Americans, and many Euro-American females) share some general characteristics of learning that differ in general from western peoples (Euro-American, primarily male, and highly acculturated minorities).

Nonwestern cultures tend to emphasize field-dependence. Individuals from these cultures perform better on verbal tasks, value harmony and cooperation, engage in relational and holistic thinking, are socially oriented, and tend to incorporate the affective self into their cognitive evaluation of reality. Western cultures traditionally have emphasized field-independence; that is, individuals perform best on analytic tasks, seek to master and control nature, value individual competition and achievement, engage in more dualistic thinking, and limit affective expression. These cultural differences not only produce different learning styles, but also influence the more subtle aspects of perception and cognitive behavior.

Students who match the instructor's style are apt to feel most comfortable and be most successful in class.

Implications for Learning

Professor Robertson's classroom capitalizes on the assimilator's style of learning. Students who are assimilators respond more easily to Robertson's style of relaxed banter in the classroom and perform better on his examinations. Although Robertson's style may have worked well at a time when students were more homogeneous, it does not work well in contemporary society, where diversity is common. Increasingly, his classes include women, minority students, and international students whose learning styles and behaviors in the classroom are different. To engage a broader array of students in his classes, Robertson should incorporate approaches that capitalize on a greater variety of learning styles.

School environments historically have valued and reinforced the cognitive learning style associated with western culture while often misconstruing nonwestern styles as deficient (J. Anderson 1988). Subsequently, students of color frequently encounter difficulties when they attempt to adapt their styles to the abstract, field-independent, analytical style of the academic classroom, especially in mathematics and the hard sciences where teaching abstract theory precedes any practical application or direct, physical experience, such as laboratory experiments. A learning approach in which direct experience precedes, rather than follows, discussion of formal concepts and theories appears to better coincide with nonwestern cognitive styles.

It is not surprising that faculty create learning environments in the classroom that reflect their own learning styles and those traditionally honored in western culture. By incorporating into the curriculum learning activities that are more inclusive of the entire range of learning styles, however, faculty can provide opportunities for more students to succeed and better prepare students for the workplace. Field-dependent learners, for example, may more easily grasp theories and concepts when they are introduced by concrete examples drawn from everyday experiences. By using classroom situations that emphasize the development of skills like contemplation and risk rather than those like speed and efficiency favored in most traditional classrooms, we can capitalize on the cultural and cognitive assets of more students at the same time we prepare students as a whole for 21st century workplaces (Stage and Manning 1992).

Research focusing on Gardner's theory of multiple intelligences is meager. Possible research questions cover a wide range. Do college students represent the full range of intelligences described by Gardner? Is it possible to modify curricula and course requirements to capitalize on the full range of intelligences? Do such modifications make a difference in students' learning? Although the review in this section describes a host of work conducted on the learning styles of college students, some of our most important questions remain only partly answered or not answered at all. Can an awareness of learning style improve college students' performance? Can teaching to a variety of learning styles improve overall learning for a college class? Could a class in learning skills develop multiple learning strengths for a college student that would improve academic success?

Conclusion
Theories of multiple intelligences (Gardner 1983) and learning styles (J. Anderson 1988; Kolb 1981) hold promise for those who hope to challenge assumptions of traditional classrooms. As we move toward learning-centered classes, these theories can inspire us to develop new ways to help college students to learn and prompt new questions about learning.

A NEED FOR CLASSROOM-BASED RESEARCH

Theories of motivation and learning provide numerous possibilities for research relevant to the college classroom. For the concepts and theories described in previous sections, extant research ranges from a few studies and speculative articles (Friere's conscientization) to several hundred articles focusing on college students (Kolb's learning styles). Nevertheless, even more work is needed that focuses on the effects of using exercises that appeal to a variety of learning styles in the college classroom. The purpose of this section is to provide the reader with explicit detailed information about the status of research on college students relative to the academic classroom and to identify specific research needed. Table 1 summarizes the status of research on college students with regard to each major theory delineated in this monograph and provides a guide for those interested in conducting research on learning. The first

TABLE 1

Status of Research on Specific Theories of Learning

	Verification/ Validation	College Students		Pedagogical Modification	Effects of Application	Needed Research
		Class	*Cohort*			
Attribution	E	M	L	L	L	Gender, ethnicity, students' behavior, classroom learning
Self-efficacy	E	M	M	L	L	Instructor's beliefs, students' behavior, classroom learning
Social Constructivism	L	L	L	L	L	Gender, ethnicity, roles, behaviors, classroom learning
Conscientization	L	L	L	L	L	Verify and describe pedagogy, classroom learning
Learning Styles	E	E	L	E	L	Choice of career, differences, classroom learning
Multiple Intelligences	L	L	L	L	L	Verify and describe pedagogy, classroom learning

E = extensive, M = moderate, L = limited.

column indicates the amount of research conducted on a topic in general, the second and third columns the amount focusing on college students and whether the studies were performed on large cohorts or a classroom, the fourth and fifth columns whether pedagogical modifications based on the theory have been attempted and whether the applications were effective, and the last column a recommended direction for research.

Attribution Theory

Attribution theory has been applied to achievement and learning since the 1970s. Although extensive research establishes that college students predominantly attribute successes and failures to effort and ability, more research is needed on Weiner's classification of underlying dimensions for causes of success and failure (see Weiner 1986). Several instruments exist for measuring causal attributions, including the Attributional Style Questionnaire (C. Peterson, Semmel, von Baeyer, Abramson, Metalsky, and Seligman 1982) and the Attributional Style Assessment Test (Anderson, Horowitz, and French 1983). The Multidimensional/Multiattributional Causality Scale (Lefcourt, von Baeyer, Ware, and Cox 1979), specifically designed for use with college students, has been refined four times.

Most studies of attribution focus on younger students, but applications to college populations and college classrooms are increasing. The research increasingly is moving into regular classroom interactions and other aspects of actual teaching and learning situations. Research on pedagogical modifications is limited, but as the importance of attributions becomes more widely recognized, researchers have begun to investigate the possibility of attributional retraining for students. Trained professionals have conducted attributional retraining in counseling sessions, but more informal use by faculty and teachers in classrooms is currently being advocated, with a particular focus on how faculty give feedback on performance to students.

Some researchers are developing test/retest experiments with attributional retraining, but little longitudinal work on causal attributions has been carried out to date. Research is just beginning on whether causal attributions can be modified, how effective the modifications are with regard to subsequent achievement, the duration of effects, and whether effects of modification are greater for certain subgroups of students or under certain classroom conditions.

Possible new directions for research include:

- Exploration of the effects of causal attributions on students' learning behaviors (e.g., how causal attributions affect students' help-seeking patterns and the use of study strategies);
- Examination of attributions as one component of a causal integrated model of self-regulated learning incorporating cognition, emotions, study skills and strategies, and meta-cognition;
- Continued work on the role of causal attributions in models of learning that emphasize locus of control;
- Examination of the relationships between out-of-class campus experiences and classroom conditions and students' attributions for success.

Self-efficacy

Since Bandura's introduction of the theory of self-efficacy in the late 1970s, self-efficacy has been extensively explored in K–12 academic settings. The construct of self-efficacy (on the part of students as well as of teachers) has been successfully and consistently related to achievement. Of scores of instruments used to measure precollege self-efficacy, several have been adapted for use at the college level.

Some instruments have been devised to focus on domain-specific beliefs for college students, such as math (Hackett 1985; Hackett and Betz 1989; Kloosterman and Stage 1992; Stage and Kloosterman 1995) or science and engineering (De-Boer 1986; Lent, Brown, and Larkin 1984). Moreover, several scales were designed specifically to measure efficacy for general academic skills (see, e.g., the Self-efficacy for Learning and Performance subscale in Pintrich, Smith, Garcia, and Mc-Keachie 1991 and the Self-regulated Learning Inventory in Lindner, Harris, and Gordon 1996).

Research in the last decade has demonstrated important relationships between self-efficacy and achievement in college. Most of those studies have focused on a single course, but a few have examined self-efficacy for a broader range of students. Additionally, a small amount of research has demonstrated relationships between self-efficacy and behaviors like study strategies. While some writers have speculated on the usefulness of focus on self-efficacy for instructors, attempts to modify beliefs about self-efficacy go largely untested. Apparently, no research has examined instructors' beliefs about students' achievements in their college classes.

Possible directions for future research are similar to those for attribution theory:

- Examination of instructors' beliefs about their own ability to teach and about their students' abilities to learn and the success of students in their classes;
- Continued examination of possible relationships between students' beliefs and learning behaviors and whether those beliefs differ by gender and ethnicity;
- Examination of the ways beliefs about self-efficacy are related to choice of major and study habits;
- Examination of self-efficacy within a causal model of self-regulated learning incorporating cognition, emotions, study skills and strategies, and metacognition.

Social Constructivism

Because social constructivism is relatively new on the educational scene, it is not surprising that only limited research exists. In part because research on social constructivism is complicated by the difficulty associated with examining learning in a social context rather than an individual basis, few pure examples exist of the approach in the research. What research has been conducted tends to concentrate on specific aspects of social constructivism (e.g., peer group work) instead of a broad application of the approach and its influence on students' learning.

Research on social constructivist approaches to learning is more likely to be associated with K–12 education than higher education. Studies of social constructivism in kindergarten through grade 12 tend to focus on the role of the social dimension in individual processes of cognitive construction, collaboration as a source of learning, and the examination of the concept of cognitive apprenticeship. Research on social constructivist approaches and postsecondary education has been addressed, at least indirectly. A few aspects of the theory represented in research include peer learning, collaborative learning, problem-based learning, and the understanding that develops as part of enculturation into a community of practice.

Social constructivist approaches to learning have had their greatest influence on pedagogical innovations in postsecondary education. Although limited research exists about the impact of collaborative learning on college students, researchers seem to agree that collaborative learning positively contributes to students' learning and achievement. Examinations of the influence of collaborative learning in college support the facilitating effects of peer interaction in learning (see, e.g., Dimant and Bearison 1991; Gerlach 1994; Johnson, Johnson, and Smith 1991; Light 1990, 1992; Millis and Cottell 1998; Slavin 1995). Students who participated in collaborative learning were better able to make intellectual connections, had increased self-confidence, and valued different viewpoints (Mathews 1996). Moreover, interactions between and among students in peer learning groups generally supported students' gains in achievement (Cross and Steadman 1996). Researchers planning to explore the effects of collaborative learning on college students should consult extant work on peer collaboration among children (see Johnson and Johnson 1989; Tudge 1992).

Research on problem-based learning is meager, but it shows that as a result of participating in problem-based learning, college students perceived their learning experience was more meaningful than through conventional courses (see, e.g., Sobral 1995; Svinicki, Hagen, and Meyer 1996; Wilkerson and Gijselaers 1996). Although educators promote the usefulness of problem-based learning, research is limited on the relationship between its use in the college classroom and specific gains in students' learning.

Vygotsky's constructs, most notably the zone of proximal development, have been well received in the K–12 education community, yet his ideas remain relatively untested in postsecondary education. In addition, the cognitive apprenticeship model, whereby the student is gradually socialized into the culture of a profession or discipline, has been promoted in the literature as a valuable approach to learning about the conventions of a field or discipline, although little empirical evidence supports its influence on learning. Research aimed at studying the applicability of these two concepts to college students is warranted.

Research is needed in the following specific areas:

- Examination of social constructivism at the college level, focusing on differences among students by gender and ethnicity;
- Exploration of the extent of the influence of more skilled students on promoting understanding among all students;

Although limited research exists about the impact of collaborative learning on college students, researchers seem to agree that collaborative learning positively contributes to students' learning and achievement.

- Exploration of the use of authentic situations and problem-based learning in the promotion of learning;
- Exploration of the constructions of knowledge resulting from mutual understandings achieved in collaboration.

Conscientization

As noted, much of the literature on Freirian pedagogy consists of philosophically based discussions about Freire's liberatory ideals. Applications of Freirian pedagogy have traditionally emphasized educational practices, specifically literacy training in nonindustrialized countries. The most relevant literature regarding higher education describes approaches to curricular design and pedagological practices at the college level that would be conducive to promoting liberatory, empowering, and critical learning. Specifically, the literature regarding college-level courses tends to focus on several issues: (1) applications to ESL courses and nontraditional students; (2) resistance from both instructors and students to a Freirian approach to learning in college; and (3) Freire's ideologies and methodologies as an appropriate theoretical foundation for service-learning courses.

Much research is still needed on Freirian pedagogy in formal college education in industrialized countries, particularly:

- Purposeful attempts to verify, measure, and provide thick descriptions of conscientization as a learning process for college students;
- Studies of curricular modifications and classroom applications of Freirian pedagogy for majority college students, large lecture classes, and heterogeneous student populations;
- Continued examination of instructors' and students' resistance to Freirian pedagogy;
- Exploration of the effects of Freirian pedagogy on college students' learning.

Learning Styles

Kolb's theory of learning styles is the most examined of the theories covered in this monograph. Nevertheless, more research, incorporating newer theories and focusing more closely on classrooms, is needed. Learning styles at the college level typically are measured using Kolb's inventory of learning styles (1985). Extensive work focuses on Kolb's description of learning styles. Many researchers have undertaken validation of the theory for college students, but most research has been confined to relatively small groups. Research on large populations, such as an entire cohort of students entering a college or university, is much more limited. Extensive articles have been written about pedagogical modifications to classes, but quasi-experimental studies or case study analyses of students' achievement in those classes are almost nonexistent.

Possible future directions for research include:

- Exploration of possible relationships between learning styles and kinds of intelligence (the multiple intelligences), and choice of career or major;
- Examination of differences in performance for students whose learning style differs from the instructor's or from the majority of students in their academic environment;
- Large-scale explorations of the effects on classroom achievement when knowledge of learning styles is included in design of the curriculum.

Multiple Intelligences

The theory of multiple intelligences has limited development with regard to learning in the college classroom. The most relevant literature includes validation that various kinds of intelligence do exist among college students (Kelder 1994; Morrin 1987; Rosnow et al. 1994). The bulk of the literature describes approaches to classroom design and curriculum that would be conducive to promoting a wider range of intelligences at the college level (see, e.g., Fogarty and Stoehr 1995; Kelder 1994; King 1994; Zevik 1994).

Particular research is needed in:

- Focused attempts to validate the existence of the range of learning styles for college students on a small scale as well as with large data sets;
- Studies of curricular modifications to explore the usefulness of implementing classroom presentations and methods of students' performances capitalizing on a variety of learning styles.

Conclusion

Despite enough material on college students' learning to fill this monograph, much of the literature describes speculation about the value of the applications of these models to learning. Higher education researchers have far to go in amassing the amount of information available to precollege educators. It is hoped that faculty, other researchers, and graduate students find this material useful as they ask questions about and examine learning in the college classroom.

IMPLICATIONS FOR THE COLLEGE CLASSROOM

Although teaching and learning are inseparably linked, the connection is frequently ignored in practice. Teaching methods employed in the college classroom tend to be based on observation, modeling, trial and error, or "intuitive guesswork" rather than on theories of learning (Fincher 1994). The reverse is also true: Theories of learning are seldom linked directly to teaching approaches. This failure to explicitly link teaching and theories of learning limits our use of the vast research about learning, and impedes our ability to enhance instruction and to positively influence students' learning. This section begins to explicate the connections between teaching and theories of learning in the hope of helping educators more clearly develop a conceptual foundation for their college teaching.

As you read the theories of learning presented in the previous sections, you may have noticed the explicit connections to teaching. You may also have started drawing your own connections to teaching practices currently being discussed in the literature (see McKeachie 1994; Menges, Weimer, and Associates 1996). This section illustrates the connections between theories of learning and the implications for teaching by focusing on five approaches to teaching: collaborative learning, peer teaching, learning communities, service learning, and technology. These approaches represent some of the recent trends to incorporate active learning into instructional practice, but they are by no means the only approaches that could have been included. To illustrate the possibilities for applying theories of learning to the college classroom, each approach is paired with one theory discussed in this monograph. These associations are not meant to imply that the theories directly correspond to these teaching approaches, nor are they meant to be the only possible associations. Rather, it is hoped that when teachers think about teaching and learning in college classrooms, they continue to make connections between theories of learning and the multitude of existing and emerging approaches to teaching in the college classroom.

Collaborative Learning and Attribution Theory

Collaborative learning, an umbrella term for a variety of educational approaches involving joint intellectual effort by students, or students and instructors together, is becoming increasingly prominent in college classrooms (Smith and MacGregor 1992).

Characteristics of collaborative learning commonly include in-class or out-of-class time built around group work; students' active exploration or application of the course material, not simply the instructor's presentation of it; and students' and instructors' shared responsibility as partners in learning (Gamson 1994; Smith and MacGregor 1992). Underlying the notion of shared responsibility is the presumption that each member of the group is capable of making, and is expected to make, a valuable contribution to the endeavor.

Students and faculty working together to create knowledge in collaborative learning groups is in contrast with the traditional classroom experience where students work individually to increase their learning. Whereas a student's ability and effort are equally important in his or her individual work, ability is downplayed and effort plays a more significant role in collaborative learning groups. Although it is possible for students of high ability to perform well on the conventional measures of learning, such as in-class tests, without having expended a great deal of effort, they are unlikely to be as successful in group learning situations where the absence of effort is perhaps more apparent. Moreover, because group members share responsibility for the final product, collaborative learning appears to deemphasize competition in favor of cooperation. These features make collaborative learning situations an attractive venue through which adaptive ascriptions for performance can be encouraged.

While collaborative learning is not a new concept, our understanding of how adaptive attributions for success develop within these learning contexts is meager. Preliminary study suggests that the triadic dimensionality of Weiner's conceptualization of causal attributions (stability, controllability, and locus) is upheld in group learning (S. Peterson 1992). Not all the hypothesized relationships that have been broadly supported in individual learning situations materialized, however. For instance, as hypothesized in causal attribution theory, high-performing students who attributed success to stable causes had higher expectations for future outcomes, but, contrary to expectations, less successful achievers did not necessarily have reduced expectancy regarding their future performance after participating in a collaborative project. The relationships surrounding controllability were not supported at all. Perhaps because of students' difficulty in discerning what aspects of collaborative learning are actually within their control, the development of an internal locus of control for success was problematic. Interestingly, while 57 percent of the students cited effort as a factor responsible for their performance, only 3 percent cited ability. In addition, group dynamics, a factor not typically cited as a cause of individual performance outcomes, showed up as a causal factor for performance outcomes in 31 percent of the cases. And in collaborative learning situations as well as in more traditional classroom contexts, the way in which faculty provide feedback on performance can contribute to or detract from the formation of adaptive patterns of making causal ascriptions for performance outcomes.

An increase in the use of collaborative learning situations at the college level can be expected in the coming decade, as faculty place more emphasis on equipping graduates with the team-playing skills necessary for the world of work in the 21st century. More research on how adaptive attributions are formed in the context of collaborative learning is clearly necessary. In addition, collaborative learning, with its focus on effort, strategy, and factors other than ability, may be uniquely situated not only as a profitable, albeit underused, vehicle for learning, but also for developing and maintaining motivationally healthy attitudes about the causes of learning outcomes as well.

Peer Teaching and Self-efficacy

Peer teaching, the process of students' teaching their fellow students, is one of the oldest forms of collaborative learning (Smith and MacGregor 1992). Approaches to peer teaching have proliferated in higher education, and their designs are quite variable (see Whitman 1988). Three of the most successful and widely adapted approaches to peer teaching include supplemental instruction by an undergraduate teaching assistant; writing fellows, an approach in which upper-division students who are strong writers read and respond to the papers of all students in an undergraduate class; and mathematics workshops, an approach that focuses on small-group problem solving through peer teaching (Smith and Mac-Gregor 1992).

Unlike traditional tutoring models that focus on remediation, approaches to peer teaching whose context for learning is one of collaboration and success provide a distinct opportunity to boost a student's sense of self-efficacy. For example,

An increase in the use of collaborative learning situations at the college level can be expected in the coming decade, as faculty place more emphasis on equipping graduates with the team-playing skills necessary for the world of work in the 21st century.

the intensive mathematics workshops at the University of California–Berkeley (Treisman 1985) emphasize small-group problem solving with an explicit emphasis on peer teaching. In contrast to a traditional model of tutoring geared toward students in academic difficulty, this approach to peer teaching assumes the culture of an honors program and supplements the regular lecture and discussion sections of *all* students. The emphasis on developing strength rather than remediating weakness and on the collaboration of peers rather than competition among individuals has helped to reverse the prevailing patterns of failure in calculus classes by African-American and Latino students at Berkeley (Treisman 1985).

But how or why does this approach to teaching make a difference in students' learning? Does a connection exist between a particular learning theory, such as self-efficacy, and a method of teaching? According to Bandura (1994), for example, self-efficacy can be developed through mastery experiences, vicarious experiences, social persuasion, and somatic and emotional states. Ideally, when a learning dyad is functioning productively, a weaker student is provided the opportunity to experience success beyond his or her ability, enjoy the partner's success vicariously, be persuaded to take risks that lead to learning, and enjoy the thrill or at least the satisfaction of successful learning.

In this example, the use in the mathematics workshops of small-group problem solving explicitly emphasizing peer teaching offers opportunities for the development of positive self-efficacy in the four ways Bandura describes. Learners who believe their individual efforts will result in only mediocre performance at best or who are bored by individual learning can benefit from the group experience. The ebb and flow of ideas, the false starts of even the best students and the professor, and the humor that can come with effort to solve a problem together can all contribute to weaker students' beliefs in their own abilities. Once developed, those positive beliefs should lead to further successes, within groups and for individuals.

Technology, Learning Styles, and Multiple Intelligences

Technology is distinctive in the opportunities it provides for revamping the college classroom. Unlike the approaches discussed earlier, applications of technology, as a new phenomenon, will gain attention and use merely by existing. The likely uses of technology in the classroom have possibilities for application that benefit students with intellectual strengths as well as those with a variety of learning styles.

Obvious possible uses of technology include students' passive observation and active creation of music and videos. Music can be used to attract students to a topic, to capitalize on the strengths of students who have special talents and skills in music, and to appeal sensually and affectively to all students by creating a pleasant environment in the classroom. Similarly, videos can be used to connect abstract conceptualizations studied in class to the realities of the inner city, a campus across the country, or life on a remote island.

Likewise, students can explore topics related to material presented in class through videos. For example, one group of students created a video about the difficulties of maneuvering a wheelchair around campus for a class of future higher education administrators. Their project drove home the realities of the difference between legal compliance with the Americans with Disabilities Act and true accessibility.

Current lore from kindergarten through high school describes students who were turned off and tuned out to the experiences of a traditional classroom. Some of those students, when provided with an opportunity to work with computers, proved to be productive students and sometimes mentors for other students as well as their teachers. Many of the students, who went on to attend college, are capable of creating multimedia products focusing on a given topic, and their instructors have sometimes found such products useful for supplementing regular classroom instruction.

Many college students enjoy spending their free time engaging in chat-room conversations on the Internet. Some enterprising faculty have capitalized on these students' social habits to create chat rooms for their classes where students can exchange information and ideas outside class and further explore concepts presented in class. Such chat rooms could be useful in helping busy commuter students be connected to academics on their own schedule.

Learning Communities and Social Constructivism

"Learning community" refers to a variety of curricular models that restructure the curriculum to link courses or coursework so that a group of students participate in an integrated

Some enterprising faculty have capitalized on these students' social habits to create chat rooms for their classes where students can exchange information and ideas outside class and further explore concepts presented in class.

learning experience (Gabelnick, MacGregor, Mathews, and Smith 1990). Learning communities provide a coherent academic experience for students and encourage intellectual stimulation between students and faculty and among students (B. Smith 1991). The increasing incorporation of a variety of learning communities into institutions of higher education over the last 20 years is a result of the positive association between an enriched learning environment and critical issues such as the retention of students, improved curricula, and integrated learning experiences (Tinto, Love, and Russo 1993). The movement to increase learning communities on campus is grounded in the belief that a rich learning environment for students and faculty enhances learning.

Learning communities take four common forms: linked courses, usually connecting skill courses and content courses; clusters, in which a group of students register for three or four courses linked by a common theme; freshman interest groups, which are much like clusters except for the addition of an upper-class peer adviser; and a more fully integrated program of coordinated studies (B. Smith 1991). And the definition has been expanded to include living-learning centers (Love and Love 1995). Common to all models is the development of a community of students connected through their common participation in the curriculum. Despite its many forms, the pedagogy of learning communities generally includes collaborative learning, team teaching, interdisciplinary content, integration of skill and content, and active approaches to learning (B. Smith 1991).

Many features of learning communities are consistent with those advocated by social constructivism, but collaborative group work and peer learning undergird both. Learning communities provide opportunities for students to develop an appreciation for the perspective of others, make intellectual connections, and construct learning through dialogue (MacGregor 1991; B. Smith 1991). These characteristics reflect the social constructivist's emphasis on learning and thinking in social contexts and the belief that knowledge is created through the social processes of discussion and negotiation. Learning communities that include a peer advising component, such as freshman interest groups, additionally support the social constructivist notion of the influence of the more capable peer in facilitating learning.

Learning communities are not the only avenue through which principles of social constructivism can be incorporated into students' learning experiences. Faculty who wish to more fully embrace social constructivism are likely to adopt teaching methods that, in general, emphasize student-centered approaches, grant importance to learners' construction of meaning, and facilitate intersubjective understanding among their students.

The implications of committing to a learning community suggest that faculty should support the tenets of social constructivism. In addition, learning communities can provide an opportunity to enculturate students into a community of practice. For example, learning communities created around a specific major or discipline can enhance students' learning by providing a more integrated introduction to the conventions of the field. Moreover, learning communities like the freshman interest groups that include a peer adviser support the notion of the social constructivists that the influence of the more capable peer facilitates learning.

Service Learning and Freire's Theory of Learning

Service learning, the integration of community and public service with structured and intentional learning, is increasingly evident on college campuses where service is being directly coupled with academic courses and learning in the classroom (Markus, Howard, and King 1993). Service learning provides students with experiences that combine real community needs with intentional learning goals, conscious reflection, and critical analysis. In contrast with previous volunteer movements, service learning reframes service not as a supplement to the formal curriculum, but as a necessary component of students' learning explicitly linked to academic growth (Kendall and Associates 1990). The application of theories of learning to service learning as an approach to teaching provides insights into the cognitive development that occurs through the intentional combination of service and learning. Four theories of learning can be applied to service-learning programs: social constructivism, Kolb's learning cycle, self-efficacy, and Freire's conscientization (Muller and Stage 1998). This subsection focuses specifically on the connections between service learning and Freire's theory to better understand how learning occurs in such venues.

Some connections between a service-learning approach to teaching and Freire are immediately evident. For example, service-learning programs provide a learning context that parallels many aspects of Freire's theory about learning: Service-learning allows instructors and students to engage in dialogue, instructors and students are co-investigators in the learning process, and instructor and learner are jointly responsible for learning. The emphasis of conscientization and service-learning on critical reflection also creates a natural connection between Freire's theory and service learning.

As described earlier, Freire's conscientization describes the process by which one moves from one level of consciousness to another, achieving a deepening awareness of one's sociocultural reality (Elias 1974; Freire 1985). Service learning can provide a mechanism for moving learners from one level of consciousness to another. Placements in service-learning projects can allow students to begin the learning process within their own reality, values, and situation. Moreover, this type of critical thinking is integral to moving from one level of consciousness to another. As a result, students engaged in service-learning activities often develop an increased awareness of sociocultural situations, an increased sense of empowerment in their lives, and a depth of interpretation of problems characteristic of Freire's level of critical consciousness.

A student's depth of understanding and interpretation of the concepts presented in a course may be hampered without the service-learning approach to education (see Muller and Stage 1998 for application in the context of a particular case study). Ideas and theories may remain too abstract in a traditional course. Service learning, however, can aid learning when the service placement allows a student's learning, and process of conscientization, to begin with familiar ideas, words, and situations rather than abstract concepts and academic rhetoric. The service placement often allows students to grapple intellectually with genuine issues; it also provides an opportunity for college students to act on their beliefs.

Conclusion
The theories and models outlined in this monograph suggest various implications for college classrooms. Educators seeking to increase the breadth and depth of the theoretical framework on which they base their practice are encouraged to

...service-learning programs provide a learning context that parallels many aspects of Freire's theory about learning...

examine the links between teaching and theories of learning. As attention continues to be directed at improving teaching and students' learning in postsecondary education, educators would be wise to increase their understanding of theories of learning and how those theories can contribute to improved instruction.

CONCEPTS OF ACADEMIC LEARNING

As we move toward learning-centered campuses, the distinctions between the roles of the teacher and the learner are becoming more blurred. An ability to be a lifelong learner, a trait required for success in the 21st century, requires individuals to "teach" themselves, not simply to receive information from an external authority. More attention is being given to the conditions that foster such an attitude. And teaching students who come from a variety of cultural, economic, and academic backgrounds requires conversation among faculty about how to deal with these concerns.

While the theories and models presented in this volume emphasize different aspects of learning, they share a common characteristic. Each takes a learning-centered approach to education by regarding college classrooms from the students' vantage point, a perspective that has only recently gained the legitimacy it deserves (Barr and Tagg 1995). Using theory, this monograph demonstrates the ways learning is impacted by students' interpretations of their academic experiences—how they process information, make sense of it, and situate it in the wider context of their lives. It shows that what students believe about their personal competence for academic tasks and how they interpret their academic successes and failures affect their subsequent engagement in similar tasks and their actual learning. It is hoped that faculty will use the practical examples based on theory to structure their classrooms, their behaviors, and their commentary to enhance students' attitudes toward learning and to build students' learning skills and their confidence in using them.

Wholesale adoption of these theories would be difficult, if not impossible. Given the infinite variety of backgrounds, skills, and styles that college teachers exhibit, instructors should explore the applications suggested here to identify theories most consonant with their own strengths, their subject matter, and their students' needs. An idiosyncratic yet thoughtful approach to application, as illustrated in the examples provided, can benefit students' learning without the investment of time and energy that sweeping curricular modifications require. In the majority of cases, applying these theories relies more on a willingness by faculty and student affairs professionals to consider student-centered approaches to giving feedback on performance, structuring class formats, and conducting performance evaluations than on radical curricular change. It is hoped that faculty and administrators will think more broadly about learning from students' point of view. And if these theories prompt questioning and curiosity about learning in all its puzzling aspects, this volume will have been a success.

REFERENCES

The Educational Resources Information Center (ERIC) Clearing-house on Higher Education abstracts and indexes the current literature on higher education for inclusion in ERIC's database and announcement in ERIC's monthly bibliographic journal, *Resources in Education* (RIE). Most of these publications are available through the ERIC Document Reproduction Service (EDRS). For publications cited in this bibliography that are available from EDRS, ordering number and price code are included. Readers who wish to order a publication should write to the ERIC Document Reproduction Service, 7420 Fullerton Road, Suite 110, Springfield, Virginia 22153-2852. (Phone orders with VISA or MasterCard are taken at 800/443-ERIC or 703/440-1400.) When ordering, please specify the document (ED) number. Documents are available as noted in microfiche (MF) and paper copy (PC). If you have the price code ready when you call, EDRS can quote an exact price. The last page of the latest issue of *Resources in Education* also has the current cost, listed by code.

Abramson, Lyn, Judy Garber, and Martin Seligman. 1980. "Learned Helplessness in Humans: An Attributional Analysis." In *Human Helplessness: Theory and Applications,* edited by J. Garber and M.E.P. Seligman. New York: Academic Press.

Allen, Deborah E., Barbara J. Duch, and Susan E. Groh. 1996. "The Power of Problem-Based Learning in Teaching Introductory Science Courses." In *Bringing Problem-Based Learning to Higher Education: Theory and Practice,* edited by LuAnn Wilkerson and Wim Gijselaers. New Directions for Teaching and Learning No. 68. San Francisco: Jossey-Bass.

American Association for Higher Education. 1992. *Principles of Good Practice for Assessing Student Learning.* Washington, D.C.: Author.

American College Personnel Association. 1994. *The Student Learning Imperative: Implications for Student Affairs.* Washington, D.C.: Author.

Ames, Russell, and Sing Lau. 1982. "An Attributional Analysis of Student Help-Seeking in Academic Settings." *Journal of Educational Psychology* 74: 414–23.

Anazonwu, Charles O. 1995. "Locus of Control, Academic Self-concept, and Attribution of Responsibility for Performance in Statistics." *Psychological Reports* 77: 367–70.

Anderson, C.A., L.M. Horowitz, and R. French. 1983. "Attributional Style of Lonely and Depressed People." *Journal of Personality and Social Psychology* 45: 127–36.

Anderson, Craig A., and Dennis Jennings. 1980. "When Experiences of Failure Promote Expectations of Success: The Impact of Attributing Failure to Ineffective Strategies." *Journal of Personality* 48: 393–407.

Anderson, James A. 1988. "Cognitive Styles and Multicultural Populations." *Journal of Teacher Education* 39(1): 2–9.

Arkin, Robert M., and Ann Baumgardner. 1985. "Self-handicapping." In *Attribution: Basic Issues and Applications,* edited by J.H. Harvey and G. Weary. Orlando: Academic Press.

Aronowitz, Stanley. 1993. "Paulo Freire's Radical Democratic Humanism." In *Paulo Freire: A Critical Encounter,* edited by Peter McLaren and Peter Leonard. London: Routledge.

Astin, Alexander. 1984. "Student Involvement: A Developmental Theory for Higher Education." *Journal of College Student Development* 25: 297–308.

———. 1993. *What Matters in College? Four Critical Years Revisited.* San Francisco: Jossey-Bass.

Astin, Helen. 1985. "Providing Incentives for Teaching Underprepared Students." *Educational Record* 66(1): 26–29.

Ausubel, D.P. 1963. *The Psychology of Meaningful Verbal Learning.* New York: Grune & Stratton.

Bandura, Albert. 1965. "Vicarious Processes: A Case of No-Trial Learning." In *Advances in Experimental Social Psychology,* vol. 2, edited by L. Berkowitz. New York: Academic Press.

———. 1977. "Self-efficacy: Toward a Unifying Theory of Behavior Change." *Psychological Review* 84: 191–215.

———. 1986. *Social Foundations of Thought and Action: A Social Cognitive Theory.* Englewood Cliffs, N.J.: Prentice-Hall.

———. 1993. "Perceived Self-efficacy in Cognitive Development and Functioning." *Educational Psychologist* 28: 117–48.

———. 1994. "Self-efficacy." In *Encyclopedia of Human Behavior,* vol. 4, edited by V.S. Ramachaudran. New York: Academic Press.

———. 1997. *Self-efficacy: The Exercise of Control.* New York: Freeman.

Bandura, Albert, and R. Walters. 1963. *Social Learning and Personality Development.* New York: Holt, Rinehart & Winston.

Banning, James H. 1989. "Creating a Climate for Successful Student Development: The Campus Ecology Model." In *Student Services: A Handbook for the Profession,* edited by U. Delworth, G. Hanson, and Associates. 2d ed. San Francisco: Jossey-Bass.

Barr, Robert B., and John Tagg. 1995. "From Teaching to Learning: A New Paradigm for Undergraduate Education." *Change* 27(6): 12–25.

Barrows, Howard S. 1996. "Problem-Based Learning in Medicine and Beyond: A Brief Overview." In *Bringing Problem-Based*

Learning to Higher Education: Theory and Practice, edited by LuAnn Wilkerson and Wim Gijselaers. New Directions for Teaching and Learning No. 68. San Francisco: Jossey-Bass.

Basow, Susan A., and Kristi Medcalf. 1988. "Academic Achievement and Attributions among College Students: Effects of Gender and Sex Typing." *Sex Roles* 19: 555–67.

Baxter-Magolda, Marcia. 1990. "Gender Differences in Epistemological Development." *Journal of College Student Development* 31(6): 555–61.

Berger, Peter, and Thomas Luckmann. 1966. *The Social Construction of Reality.* Garden City, N.Y.: Doubleday.

Bergeron, Lynn M., and John L. Romano. 1994. "The Relationships among Career Decision Making, Self-efficacy, Educational Indecision, Vocational Indecision, and Gender." *Journal of College Student Development* 35: 19–24.

Best, Linda. 1990. "Freire's Liberatory Learning: A New Pedagogy Reflecting Traditional Beliefs." ED 326 050. 30 pp. MF–01; PC–02.

Billson, J.M., and R.G. Tiberius. 1991. "Effective Social Arrangements for Teaching and Learning." In *College Teaching: From Theory to Practice,* edited by R.J. Menges and M.D. Svinicki. New Directions for Teaching and Learning No. 45. San Francisco: Jossey-Bass.

Blake, J. Herman. 1985. "Approaching Minority Students as Assets." *Academe* 71(6): 19–21.

Blimling, Gregory S., and John H. Schuh. 1981. *Increasing the Educational Role of Residence Halls.* New Directions for Student Services No. 13. San Francisco: Jossey-Bass.

Blumenfeld, Phyllis C., Ronald Marx, Elliot Soloway, and Joseph Krajcik. November 1996. "Learning with Peers: From Small-group Cooperation to Collaborative Communities." *Educational Researcher* 25(8): 37–40.

Bodi, Sonia. 1990. "Teaching Effectiveness and Bibliographic Instruction: The Relevance of Learning Styles." *College and Research Libraries* 51: 113–19.

Boerckel, Denise, and Chris Barnes. 1991. "Defeating the Banking Concept of Education: An Application of Paulo Freire's Methodologies." Paper presented at an annual meeting of the College English Association, San Antonio, Texas. ED 340 017. 13 pp. MF–01; PC–01.

Borkowski, John G., Martha Carr, Elizabeth Rellinger, and M. Pressley. 1990. "Self-regulated Cognition: Interdependence of Metacognition Attributions and Self-esteem." In *Dimensions of Thinking and Cognitive Instruction,* edited by B.F. Jones and L.

Idol. Hillsdale, N.J.: Erlbaum.

Borkowski, J.G., and P.K. Thorpe. 1994. "Self-regulation and Motivation: A Life-Span Perspective on Underachievement." In *Self-regulation of Learning and Performance: Issues and Educational Applications,* edited by D.H. Schunk and B.J. Zimmerman. Hillsdale, N.J.: Erlbaum.

Boyatzis, Richard E., and David A. Kolb. 1991. "Assessing Individuality in Learning: The Learning Skills Profile." *Educational Psychology* 11: 279–95.

Boyer, Ernest. 1990. *Scholarship Reconsidered: Priorities of the Professoriate.* Princeton, N.J.: Carnegie Foundation for the Advancement of Teaching. ED 326 149. 151 pp. MF–01; PC not available EDRS.

Brooks, Jacqueline G., and M.G. Brooks. 1993. *In Search of Understanding: The Case for Constructivist Classrooms.* Alexandria, Va.: Association for Supervision and Curriculum Development. ED 366 428. 143 pp. MF–01; PC not available EDRS.

Brooks, Linda, Allen Cornelius, Ellen Greenfield, and Robin Joseph. 1995. "The Relation of Career-Related Work or Internship Experiences to the Career Development of College Seniors." *Journal of Vocational Behavior* 46: 332–49.

Brown, John S., Allan Collins, and Paul Duguid. 1989. "Situated Cognition and the Culture of Learning." *Educational Researcher* 18(1): 32–42.

Brown, Robert. 1968. "Manipulation of the Environmental Press in a College Residence Hall." *Personnel and Guidance Journal* 46: 555–60.

———. 1989. "Fostering Intellectual and Personal Growth: The Student Development Role." In *Student Services: A Handbook for the Profession,* edited by Ursula Delworth, Gary Hanson, and Associates. 2d ed. San Francisco: Jossey-Bass.

Bruffee, K.A. 1993. *Collaborative Learning: Higher Education, Interdependence, and the Authority of Knowledge.* Baltimore: Johns Hopkins Univ. Press.

Bruner, Jerome S., J.J. Goodnow, and G.A. Austin. 1956. *A Study of Thinking.* New York: Wiley.

Bruning, R.H. 1994. "The College Classroom from the Perspective of Cognitive Psychology." In *Handbook of College Teaching: Theory and Applications,* edited by K.W. Prichard and R.M. Sawyer. Westport, Conn.: Greenwood Press.

Busch, Tor. 1995. "Gender Differences in Self-efficacy and Attitudes toward Computers." *Journal of Educational Computing Research* 12: 147–58.

Carr, Martha, John Borkowski, and Scott Maxwell. 1991. "Motivational Components of Underachievement." *Developmental Psychology* 27: 108–18.

Cavanaugh, Stephen, et al. 1995. "The Assessment of Student Nurse Learning Styles Using the Kolb Learning Inventory." *Nurse Education Today* 15(3): 177–83.

Chickering, Arthur W. 1969. *Education and Identity.* San Francisco: Jossey-Bass.

Chickering, Arthur W., and Zelda F. Gamson. 1987. "Seven Principles for Good Practice in Undergraduate Education." *AAHE Bulletin* 39(7): 3–7.

Claxton, Charles S., and Patricia H. Murrell. 1987. *Learning Styles: Implications for Improving Educational Practices.* ASHE-ERIC Higher Education Report No. 4. Washington, D.C.: Association for the Study of Higher Education. ED 293 478. 116 pp. MF–01; PC–05.

Cobb, Paul. 1994a. "Constructivism in Mathematics and Science Education." *Educational Researcher* 23(7): 4.

———. 1994b. "Where Is the Mind? Constructivist and Sociocultural Perspectives on Mathematical Development." *Educational Researcher* 23(7): 13–20.

Confrey, Jere. 1995. "How Compatible Are Radical Constructivism, Sociocultural Approaches, and Social Constructivism?" In *Constructivism in Education,* edited by Leslie Steffe and Jerry Gale. Hillsdale, N.J.: Erlbaum.

Cooper, James L. 1995. "Cooperative Learning and Critical Thinking." *Teaching of Psychology* 22(1): 7–9.

Cornwell, J.M., and P.A. Manfredo. 1994. "Kolb's Learning Style Theory Revisited." *Educational and Psychological Measurement* 54: 317–27.

Covington, Martin V. 1992. *Making the Grade: A Self-worth Perspective on Motivation and School Reform.* Cambridge: Cambridge Univ. Press.

Covington, Martin V., and Carol Omelich. 1979. "Effort: The Double-edged Sword in School Achievement." *Journal of Educational Psychology* 71: 169–82.

———. 1981. "As Failures Mount: Affective and Cognitive Consequences of Ability Demotion in the Classroom." *Journal of Educational Psychology* 73: 796–808.

Cromwell, R. 1994. "Creativity Enhances Learning in College Classes: The Importance of Artists and Poets." In *Theories of Learning: Teaching for Understanding and Creativity,* edited by R. Kelder. New Paltz, N.Y.: SUNY Conference of the Institute for the Study of Postsecondary Pedagogy. ED 394 408. 232 pp. MF–01; PC–10.

Cross, K. Patricia. 1976. *Accent on Learning: Improving Instruction and Reshaping the Curriculum.* San Francisco: Jossey-Bass.

Cross, K. Patricia, and Mimi Steadman. 1996. *Classroom Research: Implementing the Scholarship of Teaching.* San Francisco: Jossey-Bass.

Croteau, James M., and Robert B. Slaney. 1994. "Two Methods of Exploring Interests: A Comparison of Outcomes." *Career Development Quarterly* 42: 252–61.

Daniels, Harry, ed. 1996. *An Introduction to Vygotsky.* London: Routledge.

Das Gupta, Prajna, and Ken Richardson. 1995. "Theories of Cognitive Development." In *Children's Cognitive and Language Development,* edited by Victor Lee and Prajna Das Gupta. Oxford, U.K.: Blackwell.

Davis, J.R. 1993. *Better Teaching, More Learning: Strategies for Success in Postsecondary Settings.* Phoenix: Oryx Press.

Davis, Todd M., and Patricia H. Murrell. 1993. *Turning Teaching into Learning: The Role of Student Responsibility in the Collegiate Experience.* ASHE-ERIC Higher Education Report No. 8. Washington, D.C.: George Washington Univ., Graduate School of Education and Human Development. ED 372 703. 122 pp. MF–01; PC–05.

DeBoer, George E. 1985. "Success and Failure in the First Year of College: Effects of Expectations, Affect, and Persistence." *Journal of College Student Personnel* 26(3): 234–39.

———. 1986. "Perceived Science Ability as a Factor in the Course Selections of Men and Women in College." *Journal of Research in Science Teaching* 23(4): 343–52.

DeCoster, David. 1968. "Effects of Homogeneous Housing Assignments for High-ability Students." *Journal of College Student Personnel* 8: 75–78.

Delandshere, Ginette, and A.R. Petrosky. 1994. "Capturing Teachers' Knowledge: Performance Assessment." *Educational Researcher* 23(5): 11–18.

Diener, Carol I., and Carol S. Dweck. 1980. "An Analysis of Learned Helplessness: II. The Processing of Success." *Journal of Personality and Social Psychology* 39: 940–52.

Dimant, Rose J., and David J. Bearison. 1991. "Development of Formal Reasoning during Successive Peer Interactions." *Developmental Psychology* 27(2): 277–84.

Drew, David E. 1996. *Aptitude Revisited: Rethinking Math and*

Science Education for America's Next Century. Baltimore: Johns
  Hopkins Univ. Press.

Driscoll, Marcy P. 1994. *Psychology of Learning for Instruction.*
  Needham Heights, Mass.: Allyn & Bacon.

Driver, Rosalind. 1995. "Constructivist Approaches to Science
  Teaching." In *Constructivism in Education,* edited by L.P. Steffe
  and J. Gale. Hillsdale, N.J.: Erlbaum.

Driver, Rosalind, Hilary Asoko, John Leach, Eduardo Mortimer, and
  Philip Scott. 1994. "Constructing Scientific Knowledge in the
  Classroom." *Educational Researcher* 23(7): 5–12.

Dweck, Carol S., and Barbara Licht. 1980. "Learned Helplessness
  and Intellectual Achievement." In *Human Helplessness: Theory
  and Applications,* edited by J. Gerber and M. Seligman. New
  York: Academic Press.

Eccles, Jacqueline S. 1994. "Understanding Women's Educational
  and Occupational Choices: Applying the Eccles et al. Model of
  Achievement-Related Choices." *Psychology of Women Quarterly*
  18(4): 585–609.

Eccles, Jacqueline S., T. Adler, R. Futterman, S. Goff, C. Kaczala, J.
  Meece, and C. Midgley. 1983. "Expectancies, Values, and Academic Behavior." In *Achievement and Achievement Motives,*
  edited by J. Spence. San Francisco: Freeman.

Elias, John L. 1974. "Social Learning and Paulo Freire." *Journal of
  Educational Thought* 8(1): 5–14.

Enns, Carolyn Z. 1993. "Integrating Separate and Connected Knowing: The Experimental Learning Model." *Teaching of Psychology*
  20: 7–13.

Ernest, Paul. 1995. "The One and the Many." In *Constructivism in
  Education,* edited by L.P. Steffe and J. Gale. Hillsdale, N.J.:
  Erlbaum.

Faltis, Christian. 1990. "Spanish for Native Speakers: Freirian and
  Vygotskian Perspectives." *Foreign Language Annals* 23(2):
  117–26.

Fennema, Elizabeth. 1981. "Attribution Theory and Achievement in
  Mathematics." In *The Development of Reflection,* edited by S.R.
  Yussen. New York: Academic Press.

Fincher, Cameron. 1994. "Learning Theory and Research." In
  Teaching and Learning in the College Classroom, edited by K.A.
  Feldman and M.B. Paulsen. ASHE Reader Series. Needham
  Heights, Mass.: Ginn.

Fitzgibbon, Ann. 1987. "Kolb's Experiential Learning Model as a
  Model for Supervision of Classroom Teaching for Student
  Teachers." *European Journal of Teacher Education* 10: 163–77.

Fogarty, R., and J. Stoehr. 1995. *Integrating Curricula with Multiple Intelligences: Teams, Themes, and Threads.* Palatine, Ill.: Skylight Publishing.

Forsyth, D., and J. McMillan. 1991. "Practical Proposals for Motivating Students." In *College Teaching: From Theory to Practice,* edited by R. Menges and M. Svinicki. New Directions for Teaching and Learning No. 45. San Francisco: Jossey-Bass.

Fosnot, Catherine T., ed. 1996. *Constructivism: Theory, Perspectives, and Practice.* New York: Teachers College Press.

Frankenstein, Marilyn. 1983. "Critical Mathematics Education: An Application of Paulo Freire's Epistemology." *Journal of Education* 165(4): 315–39.

Freire, Paulo. 1970a. "Cultural Action and Conscientization." *Harvard Educational Review* 40(3): 452–77.

———. 1970b. *Pedagogy of the Oppressed.* New York: Herder & Herder.

———. 1971. "To the Coordinator of a 'Cultural Circle.'" *Convergence* 4(1): 61–62.

———. 1981. "The People Speak Their Word: Learning to Read and Write in Sao Tome and Principe." *Harvard Educational Review* 51(1): 27–30.

———. 1983. "The Importance of the Act of Reading." *Journal of Education* 165(1): 5–11.

———. 1985. *An Invitation to Conscientization and Deschooling: The Politics of Education.* South Hadley, Mass.: Bergin & Garvey.

Freire, Paulo, and A. Faundez. 1989. *Learning to Question.* New York: Continuum.

Frieze, Irene H., Bernard Whitley, Barbara Hanusa, and Maureen McHugh. 1982. "Assessing the Theoretical Models for Sex Differences in Causal Attributions for Success and Failure." *Sex Roles* 8: 333–43.

Fry, Ronald, and David Kolb. 1979. "Experiential Learning Theory and Learning Experiences in Liberal Arts Education." In *Enriching the Liberal Arts through Experiential Learning,* edited by Stevens Brooks and James Althof. New Directions for Experiential Learning No. 6. San Francisco: Jossey-Bass.

Gabelnick, Faith, Jean MacGregor, Roberta Mathews, and Barbara L. Smith. 1990. *Learning Communities: Creating Connections among Students, Faculty, and Disciplines.* New Directions for Teaching and Learning No. 41. San Francisco: Jossey-Bass.

Gamson, Zelda F. 1994. "Collaborative Learning Comes of Age." *Change* 26: 44–49.

Gandara, Patricia. 1995. *Over the Ivy Walls: The Educational Mo-*

bility of Low-Income Chicanos. Social Context of Education Series. Albany, N.Y.: SUNY Press.

Gardiner, Lion. 1994. *Redesigning Higher Education: Producing Dramatic Gains in Student Learning.* ASHE-ERIC Higher Education Report No. 7. Washington, D.C.: George Washington Univ., Graduate School of Education and Human Development. ED 394 442. 233 pp. MF–01; PC–10.

Gardner, Howard. 1983. *Frames of Mind.* New York: Basic Books.

————. 1991. *The Unschooled Mind: How Children Think and How Schools Should Teach.* New York: Basic Books.

Gardner, Howard, and Thomas Hatch. 1989. "Multiple Intelligences Go to School." *Educational Researcher* 18(8): 4–9.

Garrison, Jim. 1995. "Deweyan Pragmatism and the Epistemology of Contemporary Social Constructivism." *American Educational Research Journal* 32(4): 716–40.

Garvey, Mary, et al. 1984. "An Assessment of Learning Styles among Pharmacy Students." *American Journal of Pharmaceutical Education* 48: 134–40.

Gay, Geri, and Maria Grosz-Ngate. 1994. "Collaborative Design in a Networked Multimedia Environment: Emerging Communication Patterns." *Journal of Research on Computing in Education* 26(3): 418–32.

Geiger, Marshall A., et al. 1992. "A Factor Analysis of Kolb's Revised Learning Style Inventory." *Educational and Psychological Measurement* 52: 753–59.

Gergen, Kenneth J. 1985. "The Social Constructionist Movement in Modern Psychology." *American Psychologist* 40: 266–75.

Gerlach, Jeanne M. 1994. "Is This Collaboration?" In *Collaborative Learning: Underlying Processes and Effective Techniques,* edited by Kris Bosworth and Sharon J. Hamilton. New Directions for Teaching and Learning No. 59. San Francisco: Jossey-Bass.

Gijselaers, Wim H. 1996. "Connecting Problem-Based Practices with Educational Theory." In *Bringing Problem-Based Learning to Higher Education: Theory and Practice,* edited by LuAnn Wilkerson and Wim Gijselaers. New Directions for Teaching and Learning No. 68. San Francisco: Jossey-Bass.

Gilligan, Carol. 1982. *In a Different Voice.* Cambridge, Mass.: Harvard Univ. Press.

Giroux, Henry A. 1993. "Paulo Freire and the Politics of Postcolonialism." In *Paulo Freire: A Critical Encounter,* edited by Peter McLaren and Peter Leonard. London: Routledge.

Glover, J.A., R.A. Ronning, and R.H. Bruning. 1990. *Cognitive Psychology for Teachers.* New York: Macmillan.

Gogolin, Luane, and Fred Swartz. 1992. "A Quantitative and Qualitative Inquiry into the Attitudes toward Science of Nonscience College Students." *Journal of Research in Science Teaching* 29: 5.

Goodman, N. 1986. "Mathematics as an Objective Science." In *New Direction in the Philosophy of Mathematics,* edited by T. Tymoczko. Boston: Birkhauser.

Goodsell, Anne, M. Maher, Vincent Tinto, Barbara L. Smith, and Jean MacGregor. 1992. *Collaborative Learning: A Sourcebook for Higher Education.* University Park, Penna.: National Center on Postsecondary Teaching, Learning, and Assessment.

Gould, Stephen J. 1981. *The Mismeasure of Man.* New York: Norton.

Graham, Sandra. 1990. "Communicating Low Ability in the Classroom: Bad Things Good Teachers Sometimes Do." In *Attribution Theory: Applications to Achievement, Mental Health, and Interpersonal Conflict,* edited by S. Graham and V. Folkes. Hillsdale, N.J.: Erlbaum.

Graham, Sandra, and V.S. Folkes, eds. 1990. *Attribution Theory: Applications to Achievement, Mental Health, and Interpersonal Conflict.* Hillsdale, N.J.: Erlbaum.

Graman, T. 1988. "Education for Humanization: Applying Paulo Freire's Pedagogy to Learning a Second Language." *Harvard Educational Review* 58(4): 433–48.

Greenleaf, Elizabeth A., M. Forsythe, H. Godfrey, B. Hudson, and F. Thompson. 1967. "Undergraduate Students as Members of the Residence Hall Staff." Bloomington, Ind.: National Association of Women Deans and Counselors.

Guskin, Alan E. 1997. "Restructuring to Enhance Student Learning (and Reduce Costs)." *Liberal Education* 83(2): 10–19.

Hackett, Gail. 1985. "The Role of Mathematics Self-efficacy in the Choice of Math-Related Majors of College Women and Men: A Path Analysis." *Journal of Counseling Psychology* 32: 47–56.

Hackett, Gail, and Nancy E. Betz. 1989. "An Exploration of the Mathematics Self-efficacy/Mathematics Performance Correspondence." *Journal for Research in Mathematics Education* 20(3): 261–73.

Hackett, Gail, Nancy E. Betz, J. Manuel Casas, and Indra A. Rocha-Singh. 1992. "Gender, Ethnicity, and Social Cognitive Factors Predicting the Academic Achievement of Students in Engineering." *Journal of Counseling Psychology* 39(4): 527–38.

Harlacher, E.L., and J.F. Gollattscheck. 1992. "Building Learning Communities." *Community College Review* 20(3): 29–36.

Hastie, Reid. 1984. "Causes and Effects of Causal Attribution." *Journal of Personality and Social Psychology* 46: 44–56.

Heath, Donald H. 1968. *Growing Up in College: Liberal Education and Authority*. San Francisco: Jossey-Bass.

Heath, Shirley B., and Milbrey W. McLaughlin. 1994. "Learning for Anything Everyday." *Journal of Curriculum Studies* 26: 471–89.

Heider, Fritz. 1958. *The Psychology of Interpersonal Relations*. New York: Wiley.

Heitmeyer, J.R., and H.B. Thomas. 1990. "Cognitive Learning Style Dimensions in Postsecondary Home Economics Students." *Journal of Studies in Technical Careers* 12: 139–52.

Heller, Kurt A., and Albert Ziegler. 1996. "Gender Differences in Mathematics and the Sciences: Can Attributional Retraining Improve the Performance of Gifted Females?" *Gifted Child Quarterly* 40(4): 200–210.

Henry, John W., Mark Martinko, and Margaret Pierce. 1993. "Attributional Style as a Predictor of Success in a First Computer Course." *Computers in Human Behavior* 9: 341–52.

Highhouse, Scott, and Dennis Doverspike. 1987. "The Validity of the *Learning Style Inventory 1985* as a Predictor of Cognitive Style and Occupational Preference." *Educational and Psychological Measurement* 47: 749–53.

Hilgard, E.R. 1987. *Psychology in America: A Historical Survey*. San Diego: Harcourt Brace Jovanovich.

Holland, John L. 1985. *Making Vocational Choices*. Englewood Cliffs, N.J.: Prentice-Hall.

Holley, Joyce H., and Elizabeth K. Jenkins. 1993. "The Relationship between Student Learning Style and Performance on Various Test Question Formats." *Journal of Education for Business* 68: 301–8.

Holoviak, Stephen J., et al. 1990. "Training Entrepreneurs." *Performance and Instruction* 29: 27–31.

Horn, Christy, Roger Bruning, Gregory Schraw, Ellen Curry, and Chanida Katkanant. 1993. "Paths to Success in the College Classroom." *Contemporary Educational Psychology* 18: 464–78.

Howard-Hamilton, M. 1993. "African-American Female Athletes: Issues, Implications, and Imperatives for Educators." *NASPA Journal* 30(2): 153–59.

Hudak, Mary A., and D.E. Anderson. 1990. "Formal Operations and Learning Style Predict Success in Statistics and Computer Science Courses." *Teaching of Psychology* 17: 231–34.

Jagacinski, Carolyn M., and John G. Nicholls. 1990. "Reducing Effort to Protect Perceived Ability: 'They'd Do It but I Wouldn't.'" *Journal of Educational Psychology* 82: 15–21.

Jarvis, P. 1992. *Paradoxes of Learning: On Becoming an Individual in Society*. San Francisco: Jossey-Bass.

Jaworski, Barbara. 1994. *Investigating Mathematics Teaching: A Constructivist Enquiry*. London: Falmer Press.

Johnson, David W., and Roger T. Johnson. 1989. *Cooperation and Competition: Theory and Research*. Edina, Minn.: Interaction Book Co.

Johnson, David W., Roger T. Johnson, and Karl A. Smith. 1991. *Cooperative Learning: Increasing College Faculty Instructional Productivity*. ASHE-ERIC Higher Education Report No. 4. Washington, D.C.: George Washington Univ., Graduate School of Education and Human Development. ED 343 465. 161 pp. MF–01; PC–07.

Katz, Naomi, and Nanci Heimann. 1991. "Learning Style of Students and Practitioners in Five Health Professions." *Occupational Therapy Journal of Research* 11: 238–44.

Kelder, Richard E., ed. 1994. *Theories of Learning: Teaching for Understanding and Creativity*. New Paltz, N.Y.: SUNY Conference of the Institute for the Study of Postsecondary Pedagogy. ED 394 408. 232 pp. MF–01; PC–10.

Kelly, George. 1955. *The Psychology of Personal Constructs*. New York: Norton.

Kendall, Jane C., and Associates. 1990. *Combining Service and Learning: A Resource Book for Community and Public Service*. Vols. 1 and 2. Raleigh, N.C.: National Society for Internships and Experiential Education.

King, N. 1994. "Inner Visions/Outer Versions." In *Theories of Learning: Teaching for Understanding and Creativity,* edited by R. Kelder. New Paltz, N.Y.: SUNY Conference of the Institute for the Study of Postsecondary Pedagogy. ED 394 408. 232 pp. MF–01; PC–10.

Kitchener, Karen, and Patricia King. 1990. "The Reflective Judgment Model: Ten Years of Research." In *Adult Development: Models and Methods in the Study of Adolescent and Adult Thought,* edited by M. Commons, C. Armon, L. Kohlberg, R. Richards, T. Grotzer, and J. Sinnott. New York: Praeger.

Kloosterman, Peter, and Frances K. Stage. 1992. "Measuring Beliefs about Mathematical Problem Solving." *School Science and Mathematics* 92(3): 109–15.

Kolb, David A. 1976. *Learning Style Inventory Technical Manual*. Boston: McBer & Co.

———. 1981. "Learning Styles and Disciplinary Differences." In *The Modern American College,* edited by A.W. Chickering and Associates. San Francisco: Jossey-Bass.

————. 1985. "Learning Style Inventory: Self-scoring Inventory and Interpretation Booklet." Rev. Boston: McBer & Co.

Koontz, C. 1994. "Cultivating Multiple Intelligences through 'The Living Journal.'" In *Theories of Learning: Teaching for Understanding and Creativity,* edited by R. Kelder. New Paltz, N.Y.: SUNY Conference of the Institute for the Study of Postsecondary Pedagogy. ED 394 408. 232 pp. MF–01; PC–10.

Krahe, Valerie A. 1993. "The Shape of the Container." *Adult Learning* 4: 17–18.

Krechevsky, M., and Howard Gardner. 1990. "The Emergence and Nurturance of Multiple Intelligences." In *Encouraging the Development of Exceptional Abilities and Talents,* edited by J.A. Howe. Leicester: British Psychological Society.

Kruzich, Jean M., et al. 1986. "Assessment of Student and Faculty Learning Styles: Research and Application." *Journal of Social Work Education* 22: 22–30.

Kuh, George, John Schuh, Elizabeth Whitt, and Associates. 1991. *Involving Colleges.* San Francisco: Jossey-Bass.

Laschinger, Heather K., and Marvin K. Boss. 1989. "Learning Styles of Baccalaureate Nursing Students and Attitudes toward Theory-Based Nursing." *Journal of Professional Nursing* 5: 224–30.

Lassan, Rebecca. 1984. "Learning Style Differences: Registered Nurse Students vs. Generic Student Nurses at the Baccalaureate Level." ED 240 318. 29 pp. MF–01; PC–02.

Lave, Jean. 1988. *Cognition in Practice: Mind, Mathematics, and Culture in Everyday Life.* New York: Cambridge Univ. Press.

Lefcourt, Herbert M., C.L. von Baeyer, E.E. Ware, and D.J. Cox. 1979. "The Multidimensional/Multiattributional Causality Scale." *Canadian Journal of Behavioral Science* 11: 286–304.

Leifer, A. 1972. "Ethnic Patterns in Cognitive Tasks." *Proceedings of the Annual Convention of the American Psychological Association* 7: 73–74.

Lent, R.W., S.P. Brown, and K.C. Larkin. July 1984. "Relation of Self-efficacy Expectations to Academic Achievemnt and Persistence." *Journal of Counseling Psychology* 31(3): 356–62.

Lent, R.W., F.G. Lopez, and K.J. Bieschle. 1993. "Predicting Mathematics-Related Choice and Success Behaviors: Test of an Expanded Social Cognitive Model." *Journal of Vocational Behavior* 42: 223–36.

Lerman, Stephen. 1996. "Intersubjectivity in Mathematics Learning: A Challenge to the Radical Constructivist Paradigm?" *Journal for Research in Mathematics Education* 27(2): 133–50.

Lesser, Gerald S., Gordon Fifer, and Donald H. Clark. 1965. "Mental

Abilities of Children from Different Social Class and Cultural Groups." *Monograph for the Society of Research in Child Development*. Chicago: Univ. of Chicago Press.

Licht, Barbara G., and Carol Dweck. 1983. "Sex Differences in Achievement Orientations: Consequences for Academic Choices and Attainments." In *Sex Differentiation and Schooling,* edited by M. Marland. London: Heinemann Educational Books.

Light, Richard J. 1990. *The Harvard Assessment Seminars*. Cambridge, Mass.: Harvard Univ. Press.

————. 1992. *The Harvard Assessment Seminars*. Cambridge, Mass.: Harvard Univ. Press.

Lindner, Reinhard W., and Bruce R. Harris. 1992. "Self-regulated Learning: Its Assessment and Instructional Implications." *Educational Research Quarterly* 16(2): 29–37.

Lindner, Reinhard W., Bruce R. Harris, and Wayne I. Gordon. 1996. "The Design and Development of the Self-regulated Learning Inventory: A Status Report." Paper presented at an annual meeting of the American Educational Research Association, April 8–12, New York, New York. ED 401 321. 15 pp. MF–01; PC–01.

Logan, Elisabeth. 1990. "Cognitive Styles and Online Behavior of Novice Searchers." *Information Processing and Management* 26: 503–10.

Lou, Yiping, Philip Abrami, John Spence, Catherine Poulsen, Bette Chambers, and Sylvia d'Apollonia. 1996. "Within-class Grouping." *Review of Educational Research* 66(4): 423–58.

Love, Anne Goodsell, and Patrick G. Love. 1995. *Enhancing Student Learning: Intellectual, Social, and Emotional Integration*. ASHE-ERIC Higher Education Report No. 4. Washington, D.C.: George Washington Univ., Graduate School of Education and Human Development. ED 400 742. 166 pp. MF–01; PC–07.

Lucas, Ann F. 1990. "Using Psychological Models to Understand Student Motivation." In *The Changing Face of College Teaching,* edited by M.D. Svinicki. New Directions for Teaching and Learning No. 42. San Francisco: Jossey-Bass.

Luzzo, Darrell A. 1993. "Reliability and Validity Testing of the Career Decision-Making Self-efficacy Scale." *Measurement and Evaluation in Counseling and Development* 26: 137–42.

————. 1994. "Assessing the Value of Social-Cognitive Constructs in Career Development." Paper presented at the 1994 Annual Convention of the American Psychological Association, Los Angeles, California.

————. 1995. "The Relative Contributions of Self-efficacy and Locus of Control to the Prediction of Career Maturity." *Journal of Col-*

lege Student Development 36: 61–66.

Luzzo, Darrell A., and Barbara E. Ward. 1995. "The Relative Contributions of Self-efficacy and Locus of Control to the Prediction of Vocational Congruence." *Journal of Career Development* 21: 307–17.

MacGregor, Jean. 1990. "Collaborative Learning: Shared Inquiry as a Process of Reform." In *The Changing Face of College Teaching,* edited by M.D. Svinicki. New Directions for Teaching and Learning No. 42. San Francisco: Jossey-Bass.

———. 1991. "What Difference Do Learning Communities Make?" *Washington Center NEWS* 6(1): 4–9. Olympia, Wash.: Evergreen State College, Washington Center for Undergraduate Education.

McHugh, Maureen, Irene H. Frieze, and Barbara H. Hanusa. 1982. "Attributions and Sex Differences in Achievement: Problems and New Perspectives." *Sex Roles* 8: 467–79.

McKeachie, Wilbur J. 1994. *Teaching Tips: Strategies, Research, and Theory for College and University Teachers.* 9th ed. Lexington, Mass.: D.C. Heath.

McKeachie, Wilbur J., Paul R. Pintrich, Yi-Guang Lin, David A.F. Smith, and Rajeev Sharma. 1990. *Teaching and Learning in the College Classroom: A Review of the Research Literature.* 2d ed. Ann Arbor: Regents of the Univ. of Michigan.

McMillan, J., and D. Forsyth. 1991. "What Theories of Motivation Say about Why Learners Learn." In *College Teaching: From Theory to Practice,* edited by R. Menges and M. Svinicki. New Directions for Teaching and Learning No. 45. San Francisco: Jossey-Bass.

McNeill, Joyce H., and Pamela K. Payne. 1996. "Cooperative Learning Groups at the College Level: Applicable Learning." Paper presented at the International Early Childhood Conference on Children with Special Needs, Phoenix, Arizona. ED 404 920. 11 pp. MF–01; PC–01.

Malone, J.A., and P.C.S. Taylor, eds. 1993. *Constructivist Interpretations of Teaching and Learning Mathematics.* Perth, Australia: Curtin Univ. of Technology, National Key Centre for Teaching and Research in School Science and Mathematics.

Manning, Kathleen. 1994. "Liberation Theology and Student Affairs." *Journal of College Student Development* 35(2): 94–97.

Margetson, Don. 1994. "Current Educational Reform and the Significance of Problem-Based Learning." *Studies in Higher Education* 19(1): 5–19.

Mark, Michael, and Betty Menson. 1982. "Using David Kolb's Experiential Learning Theory in Portfolio Development Courses."

In *Building on Experiences in Adult Development,* edited by Betty Menson. New Directions for Experiential Learning No. 16. San Francisco: Jossey-Bass.

Markus, Gregory B., Jeffrey P.F. Howard, and David C. King. 1993. "Integrating Community Service and Classroom Instruction Enhances Learning: Results from an Experiment." *Educational Evaluation and Policy Analysis* 15(4): 410–19.

Marsh, Herbert W. 1986. "The Self-serving Effect Bias in Academic Attributions: Its Relation to Academic Achievement and Self-concept." *Journal of Educational Psychology* 78: 190–200.

Marshall, H.H. 1992. "Seeing, Redefining, and Supporting Student Learning." In *Redefining Student Learning: Roots of Educational Change,* edited by H.H. Marshall. Norwood, N.J.: Ablex.

Maslow, Abraham H. 1954. *Motivation and Personality.* New York: Harper & Row.

Mathews, Roberta. 1996. "Collaborative Learning: Creating Knowledge with Students." In *Teaching on Solid Ground: Using Scholarship to Improve Practice,* edited by Robert J. Menges, M. Weimer, and Associates. San Francisco: Jossey-Bass.

Menec, Verena H., and Raymond P. Perry. 1995. "Disciplinary Differences in Students' Perceptions of Success: Modifying Misperceptions with Attributional Retraining." In *Disciplinary Differences in Teaching and Learning,* edited by N. Hativa and M. Marincovich. New Directions for Teaching and Learning No. 64. San Francisco: Jossey-Bass.

Menges, Robert, and Marilla D. Svinicki, eds. 1991. *College Teaching: From Theory to Practice.* New Directions for Teaching and Learning No. 45. San Francisco: Jossey-Bass.

Menges, Robert, Maryellen Weimer, and Associates. 1996. *Teaching on Solid Ground: Using Scholarship to Improve Practice.* San Francisco: Jossey-Bass.

Mentkowski, Marcia, and A. Doherty. 1984. "Abilities That Last a Lifetime: Outcomes of the Alverno Experience." *AAHE Bulletin* 36: 5–6+.

Messick, S. 1970. "The Criterion Problem in the Evaluation of Instruction: Assessing Possible, not Just Probable, Intended Outcomes." In *The Evaluation of Instruction: Issues and Problems,* edited by M. Wittrock and D. Wiley. New York: Holt.

Meyers, Chet, and Thomas B. Jones. 1993. *Promoting Active Learning: Strategies for the College Classroom.* San Francisco: Jossey-Bass.

Michaelson, L.K. 1994. "Team Learning: Making a Case for the Small-group Option." In *Handbook of College Teaching: Theory and Applications,* edited by K.W. Prichard and R.M Sawyer. Westport, Conn.: Greenwood Press.

Millar, Susan B. 1996. "New Roles for Teachers in Today's Classrooms." In *Teaching on Solid Ground: Using Scholarship to Improve Practice,* edited by R.J. Menges, M. Weimer, and Associates. San Francisco: Jossey-Bass.

Millis, Barbara J., and Philip G. Cottell. 1998. *Cooperative Learning for Higher Education Faculty.* Phoenix: ACE/Oryx Press.

Moll, L.C. 1990. *Vygotsky and Education.* Cambridge, Eng.: Cambridge Univ. Press.

Mone, M.A., D.D. Baker, and F. Jeffries. 1995. "Predictive Validity and Time Dependency of Self-efficacy, Self-esteem, Personal Goals, and Academic Performance." *Educational and Psychological Measurement* 55(5): 716–27.

Morrin, M. 1987. "Toward a Description of Some Patterns of Verbal Communication in Face-to-Face Dyads Where Instructions Are Given." Dissertation Abstracts International 49 03A. University Microfilms No. AAD88-09394.

————. 1994. "Ways of Knowing in Education and Diverse Learning Styles." In *Theories of Learning: Teaching for Understanding and Creativity,* edited by R. Kelder. New Paltz, N.Y.: SUNY Conference of the Institute for the Study of Postsecondary Pedagogy. ED 394 408. 232 pp. MF–01; PC–10.

Muller, Patricia, and Frances K. Stage. 1998. "Service Learning: Exemplifying the Connections between Theory and Practice." In *Enhancing Student Learning: Setting the Campus Context,* edited by F. Stage, L. Watson, and M. Terrell. Alexandria, Va.: ACPA Media.

Myers, Isabella. 1980. *Gifts Differing.* Palo Alto, Calif.: Consulting Psychologists Press.

Neisser, U. 1967. *Cognitive Psychology.* New York: Appleton-Century-Crofts.

Nelson-LeGall, Sharon. 1985. "Help-Seeking Behavior in Learning." *Review of Research on Education* 12: 55–90.

Nicaise, Molly, and Maribeth Gettinger. 1995. "Fostering Reading Comprehension in College Students." *Reading Psychology* 16: 283–337.

Niles, Spencer G., and Claudia J. Sowa. 1992. "Mapping the Nomological Network of Career Self-efficacy." *Career Development Quarterly* 41: 13–21.

O'Loughlin, Michael. 1990. "Teachers' Ways of Knowing: A Journal Study of Teacher Learning in a Dialogical and Constructivist Learning Environment." Paper presented at the 1990 Annual

Meeting of the American Educational Research Association, Boston, Massachusetts. ED 327 477. 43 pp. MF–01; PC–02.

Orasanu, J., C. Lee, and S. Scribner. 1979. "Free Recall: Ethnic and Economic Group." *Child Development* 50: 1100–1109.

Ormrod, Jeanne E. 1990. *Human Learning: Principles, Theories, and Educational Applications.* Columbus, Ohio: Merrill.

Pace, C. Robert. 1979. *Measuring Outcomes of College: Fifty Years of Findings and Recommendations for the Future.* San Francisco: Jossey-Bass.

———. 1990. *The Undergraduates: A Report of Their Activities and Progress in College in the 1980s.* Los Angeles: UCLA, Center for the Study of Evaluation. ED 375 701. 164 pp. MF–01; PC–07.

Pajares, Frank. 1996. "Self-efficacy Beliefs in Academic Settings." *Review of Educational Research* 66(4): 543–78.

Palmer, Parker. 1993. *To Know as We Are Known: Education as a Spiritual Journey.* San Francisco: Harper.

———. 1997. "The Heart of the Teacher." *Change* 29(6): 14–21.

Parker, Clyde. 1977. "On Modelling Reality." *Journal of College Student Personnel* 18: 419–25.

Parsons, Jacquelynne E., Judith L. Meece, Terry F. Adler, and Caroline M. Kaczala. 1982. "Sex Differences in Attributions and Learned Helplessness." *Sex Roles* 8: 421–32.

Pascarella, Ernest T. 1985. "College Environmental Influences on Learning and Cognitive Development: A Critical Review and Synthesis." In *Higher Education: Handbook of Theory and Research,* vol. 1, edited by J. Smart. New York: Agathon Press.

Pascarella, Ernest T., Marcia Edison, Linda S. Hagedorn, Amaury Nora, and Patrick T. Terenzini. 1996. "Influences on Students' Internal Locus of Attribution for Academic Success in the First Year of College." *Research in Higher Education* 37: 731–56.

Pascarella, Ernest T., and Patrick T. Terenzini. 1991. *How College Affects Students: Findings and Insights from Twenty Years of Research.* San Francisco: Jossey-Bass.

Perry, Raymond P., Frank J. Hechter, Verena H. Menec, and Leah E. Weinberg. 1993. "Enhancing Achievement Motivation and Performance in College Students: An Attributional Retraining Perspective." *Research in Higher Education* 34: 687–723.

Perry, Raymond P., and Jamie-Lynn Magnusson. 1989. "Causal Attributions and Perceived Performance: Consequences for College Students' Achievement and Perceived Control in Different Instructional Conditions." *Journal of Educational Psychology* 81: 164–72.

Perry, Raymond P., Verena H. Menec, and C. Ward Struthers. 1996.

"Student Motivation from the Teacher's Perspective." In *Teaching on Solid Ground: Using Scholarship to Improve Practice*, edited by R.J. Menges, M. Weimer, and Associates. San Francisco: Jossey-Bass.

Perry, William. 1981. "Cognitive and Ethical Growth: The Making of Meaning." In *The Modern American College*, edited by A. Chickering and Associates. San Francisco: Jossey-Bass.

Peterson, Christopher. 1990. "Explanatory Style in the Classroom and in the Playing Field." In *Attribution Theory: Applications to Achievement, Mental Health, and Interpersonal Conflict*, edited by S. Graham and V.S. Folkes. Hillsdale, N.J.: Erlbaum.

Peterson, Christopher, and Lisa Barrett. 1987. "Explanatory Style and Academic Performance among University Freshmen." *Journal of Personality and Social Psychology* 53: 603–7.

Peterson, C., A. Semmel, C. von Baeyer, I.Y. Abramson, G.I. Metalsky, and M.E.P. Seligman. 1982. "The Attributional Style Questionnaire." *Cognitive Theory and Research* 6: 287–300.

Peterson, S.E. 1992. "College Students' Attributions for Performance on Cooperative Tasks." *Contemporary Educational Psychology* 17: 114–24.

Peterson, Shari L. 1993. "Career Decision Making, Self-efficacy, and Institutional Integration of Underprepared College Students." *Research in Higher Education* 34: 659–85.

Phillips, D.C. 1995. "The Good, the Bad, and the Ugly: The Many Faces of Constructivism." *Educational Researcher* 24(7): 5–12.

Piaget, Jean. 1970. *Science of Education and the Psychology of the Child*. New York: Orion.

Pierce, Margaret A., and John W. Henry. 1993. "Attributional Style as a Predictor of Success in College Mathematics." ED 365 528. 27 pp. MF–01; PC–02.

Pintrich, Paul R. 1989. "The Dynamic Interplay of Student Motivation and Cognition in the Classroom." In *Advances in Motivations and Achievement: Motivation-Enhancing Environments*, edited by M. Maehr and C. Ames. Vol. 6. New York: JAI Press.

Pintrich, Paul R., D. Smith, T. Garcia, and W. McKeachie. 1991. *A Manual for the Use of the Motivated Strategies for Learning Questionnaire*. Ann Arbor, Mich.: National Center for the Improvement of Postsecondary Teaching and Learning.

Posey, Evelyn J. 1984. "Learning Style Inventory: Implementation Research." *Journal of Developmental and Remedial Education* 7: 16–18.

Post, Phyllis, Mac A. Stewart, and Phillip L. Smith. 1991. "Self-efficacy Interest and Consideration of Math/Science and Non–

Math/Science Occupations among Black Freshmen." *Journal of Vocational Behavior* 38: 179–86.

Prawat, Richard S. 1992. "Teachers' Beliefs about Teaching and Learning: A Constructivist Perspective." *American Journal of Education* 100: 354–95.

Prawat, Richard S., and Robert E. Floden. 1994. "Philosophical Perspectives on Constructivist Views of Learning." *Educational Psychology* 29(1): 37–48.

Pressley, M., and C.B. McCormick. 1995. *Advanced Educational Psychology for Educators, Researchers, and Policy Makers.* New York: Harper Collins.

Prichard, K.W., and R.M. Sawyer, eds. 1994. *Handbook of College Teaching: Theory and Applications.* Westport, Conn.: Greenwood Press.

Ratcliff, James L., and Associates. 1995. *Realizing the Potential: Improving Postsecondary Teaching, Learning, and Assessment.* University Park, Penna.: National Center on Postsecondary Teaching, Learning, and Assessment. ED 404 939. 55 pp. MF–01; PC–03.

Rauch, K. 1994. "The Artistic Process: A Model for Teaching and Learning." In *Theories of Learning: Teaching for Understanding and Creativity,* edited by R. Kelder. New Paltz, N.Y.: SUNY Conference of the Institute for the Study of Postsecondary Pedagogy. ED 394 408. 232 pp. MF–01; PC–10.

Rega, B. 1993. "Fostering Creativity in Advertising Students: Incorporating the Theories of Multiple Intelligences and Integrative Learning." Paper presented at the 1993 Annual Meeting of the Association for Education in Journalism and Mass Communication, Kansas City, Missouri. ED 362 906. 24 pp. MF–01; PC–01.

Relich, Joseph D., Ray L. Debus, and Richard Walker. 1986. "The Mediating Role of Attribution and Self-efficacy Variables for Treatment Effects on Achievement Outcomes." *Contemporary Educational Psychology* 11: 195–216.

Rendon, Laura. 1994. "Validating Culturally Diverse Students: Toward a New Model of Learning and Student Development." *Innovative Higher Education* 19(1): 33–51.

Resnick, Lauren B. 1987. "Learning in School and Out." *Educational Researcher* 16(9): 13–20.

———. 1991. "Shared Cognition: Thinking as Social Practice." In *Perspectives on Socially Shared Cognition,* edited by Lauren B. Resnick, John M. Levine, and Stephanie D. Teasley. Washington, D.C.: American Psychological Association.

Rhoads, Robert A. 1997. *Community Service and Higher Learning:*

Explorations of the Caring Self. Albany, N.Y.: SUNY Press.

Rhoads, Robert A., and James R. Valadez. 1996. *Democracy, Multiculturalism, and the Community College.* New York: Garland Publishing.

Rogoff, Barbara. 1990. *Apprenticeship in Thinking: Cognitive Development in Social Contexts.* New York: Oxford.

Rooney, Rebecca A., and Samuel H. Osipow. 1992. "Task-Specific Occupational Self-efficacy Scale: The Development and Validation of a Prototype." *Journal of Vocational Behavior* 40: 14–32.

Rosnow, R.L., et al. 1994. "Intelligence and the Epistemics of Interpersonal Acumen: Testing Some Implications of Gardner's Theory." *Intelligence* 19: 93–116.

Rothschadl, Ann M., and Ruth V. Russell. 1992. "Improving Teaching Effectiveness: Addressing Modes of Learning in the College Classroom." *Schole: A Journal of Recreation, Education, and Leisure Studies* 7: 24–35.

Russell, Ruth V., and Ann M. Rothschadl. 1991. "Learning Styles: Another View of the College Classroom?" *Schole: A Journal of Recreation, Education, and Leisure Studies* 6: 34–45.

Ryckman, David B., and Percy D. Peckham. 1987. "Gender Differences in Attributions for Success and Failure." *Journal of Early Adolescence* 7(1): 47–63.

Sadler, Georgia R., et al. 1978. "Learning Styles and Teaching Implications." *Journal of Medical Education* 53: 847–49.

Scheye, Paula A., and Faith D. Gilroy. 1994. "College Women's Career Self-efficacy and Educational Environments." *Career Development Quarterly* 42: 244–51.

Schmitz, Bernhard, and Ellen Skinner. 1993. "Perceived Control Effort and Academic Performance: Interindividual, Intraindividual, and Multivariate Time-Series Analyses." *Journal of Personality and Social Psychology* 64(6): 1010–28.

Schroeder, Charles C. 1973. "Sex Differences and Growth toward Self-actualization during the Freshman Year." *Psychological Reports* 32: 416–18.

———. Fall 1988. "Student Affairs—Academic Affairs: Opportunities for Bridging the Gap." *ACPA Developments.*

———. 1993. "New Students—New Learning Styles." *Change* 25(4): 21–26.

Schroeder, Charles C., and A. Belmonte. 1979. "The Influence of Residential Environment on Prepharmacy Student Achievement and Satisfaction." *Journal of Pharmaceutical Education* 43: 16–19.

Schroeder, Charles C., and Phyllis Mable. 1994. *Realizing the Educational Potential of Residence Halls.* San Francisco: Jossey-Bass.

Schunk, Dale H. 1982. "Effects of Attributional Feedback on Children's Perceived Self-efficacy and Achievement." *Journal of Educational Psychology* 74: 548–56.

Seal, D.O. 1995. "Creativity, Curiosity, Exploded Chickens." *College Teaching* 43: 3–6.

Sexton, Thomas L., and Bruce W. Tuckman. 1991. "Self-beliefs and Behavior: The Role of Self-efficacy and Outcome Expectation over Time." *Personality and Individual Difference* 12(7): 725–36.

Shade, B.J. 1992. "African-American Cognitive Style: A Variable in School Success?" *Review of Educational Research* 52(2): 219–44.

Shapiro, H. 1966. "Perceptual Categorization of Lower- and Middle-Class Negro School Children." *Journal of Negro Education* 35: 218–29.

Sherkat, Darren E., and T. Jean Blocker. 1993. "Environmental Activism in the Protest Generation: Differentiating 1960s Activists." *Youth and Society* 25: 140–61.

———. 1994. "The Political Development of Sixties Activists: Identifying the Influence of Class, Gender, and Socialization on Protest Participation." *Social Forces* 72: 821–42.

Shor, Ira. 1993. "Education Is Politics: Paulo Freire's Critical Pedagogy." In *Paulo Freire: A Critical Encounter,* edited by P. McLaren and P. Leonard. London: Routledge.

Simmons, Ada B. 1996. "Beliefs and Academic Performance of Low-achieving College Students." Unpublished doctoral dissertation, Indiana Univ.–Bloomington.

Skinner, B.F. 1953. *Science and Human Behavior.* New York: Macmillan.

———. 1968. *The Technology of Teaching.* New York: Appleton-Century-Crofts.

Slavin, Robert E. 1995. *Cooperative Learning: Theory, Research, and Practice.* 2d ed. Boston: Allyn & Bacon.

———. 1997. *Educational Psychology: Theory into Practice.* 5th ed. Needham Heights, Mass.: Allyn & Bacon.

Smith, Barbara L. 1991. "Taking Structure Seriously: The Learning Community Model." *Liberal Education* 77(2): 42–48.

Smith, Barbara L., and Jean T. MacGregor. 1992. "What Is Collaborative Learning?" In *Collaborative Learning: A Sourcebook for Higher Education,* edited by A.S. Goodsell, M.R. Maher, V. Tinto, B.L. Smith, and J.T. MacGregor. University Park, Penna.: National Center on Postsecondary Teaching, Learning, and Assessment. ED 357 705. 175 pp. MF–01; PC–07.

Smith, James M. 1994. "The Effects of Education on Computer Self-efficacy." *Journal of Industrial Teacher Education* 31: 51–65.

Sobral, D.T. 1995. "The Problem-Based Learning Approach as an Enhancement Factor of Personal Meaningfulness of Learning." *Higher Education* 29(1): 93–101.

Sohn, David. 1982. "Sex Differences in Achievement Self-attributions: An Effect Size Analysis." *Sex Roles* 8: 345–57.

Solberg, V. Scott, Karen O'Brien, Pete Villareal, Richard Kennel, and Betsey Davis. 1993. "Self-efficacy and Hispanic College Students: Validation of the College Self-efficacy Instrument." *Hispanic Journal of Behavioral Sciences* 15(1): 80–95.

Sparks, Bernard I. 1990. "The Kolb Learning Styles Inventory: Predicting Academic Potential among Optometry Students." *Journal of Optometric Education* 15: 52–55.

Spivey, Nancy N. 1995. "Written Discourse: A Constructivist Perspective." In *Constructivism in Education,* edited by Leslie P. Steffe and Jerry Gale. Hillsdale, N.J.: Erlbaum.

Sprinthall, N.A., R.C. Sprinthall, and S.N. Oja. 1993. *Educational Psychology: A Developmental Approach.* 6th ed. New York: McGraw-Hill.

Stage, Frances K. 1989. "College Outcomes and Student Development: Filling the Gaps." *Review of Higher Education* 12(3): 293–304.

———. 1991. "Common Elements of Theory: A Framework for College Student Development." *Journal of College Student Development* 32: 56–61.

———. 1996. "Setting the Context: Psychological Theories of Learning." *Journal of College Student Development* 27(2): 227–35.

Stage, Frances K., and Peter Kloosterman. 1991. "Relationships between Ability, Belief, and Achievement in Remedial College Mathematics Classrooms." *Research and Teaching in Developmental Education* 8(1): 27–36.

———. 1995. "Gender, Beliefs, and Achievement in Remedial College-Level Mathematics." *Journal of Higher Education* 66(3): 294–311.

Stage, Frances K., and Kathleen Manning. 1992. *Enhancing the Multicultural Campus Environment: A Cultural Brokering Approach.* New Directions for Student Services No. 60. San Francisco: Jossey-Bass.

Stage, Frances K., and Sue A. Maple. 1996. "Incompatible Goals: Narratives of Graduate Women in the Mathematics Pipeline." *American Educational Research Journal* 33(1): 23–51.

Stage, Frances K., and N.V. Milne. 1996. "Invisible Scholars: Students with Learning Disabilities." *Journal of Higher Education* 67(4): 426–45.

Stage, Frances K., and Patricia M. Muller. 1997. "Theories of Learning for College Students." In *Enhancing Student Learning: Setting the Campus Context,* edited by F. Stage, L. Watson, and M. Terrell. Alexandria, Va.: ACPA Media.

Steffe, Leslie P., and Jerry Gale, eds. 1995. *Constructivism in Education.* Hillsdale, N.J.: Erlbaum.

Stewart, Robert A., and K. David Roach. 1993. "Argumentativeness, Religious Orientation, and Reactions to Argument Situations Involving Religious versus Nonreligious Issues." *Communication Quarterly* 41(1): 26–39.

Stice, James E. 1987. "Using Kolb's Learning Cycle to Improve Student Learning." *Engineering Education* 77: 291–96.

Stickel, Sue A., and Rhonda M. Bonett. 1991. "Gender Differences in Career Self-efficacy: Combining a Career with Home and Family." *Journal of College Student Development* 32: 297–301.

Stinson, John E., and Richard G. Milter. 1996. "Problem-Based Learning in Business Education: Curriculum Design and Implementation Issues." In *Bringing Problem-Based Learning to Higher Education: Theory and Practice,* edited by L. Wilkerson and W. Gijselaers. New Directions for Teaching and Learning No. 68. San Francisco: Jossey-Bass.

Stipek, Deborah J. 1984. "Sex Differences in Children's Attributions for Success and Failure on Math and Spelling Tests." *Sex Roles* 11: 969–81.

Stipek, Deborah J., and J. Heidi Gralinski. 1991. "Gender Differences in Children's Achievement-Related Beliefs and Emotional Responses to Success and Failure in Math." *Journal of Educational Psychology* 83: 361–71.

Stipek, Deborah J., and Joel M. Hoffman. 1980. "Children's Achievement-Related Expectancies as a Function of Academic Performance Histories and Sex." *Journal of Educational Psychology* 72(6): 861–65.

Stodolsky, S., and G. Lesser. 1967. "Learning Patterns in the Disadvantaged." *Harvard Educational Review* 37: 546–93.

Sullins, Ellen S., et al. 1995. "Predicting Who Will Major in a Science Discipline: Expectancy–Value Theory as Part of an Ecological Model for Studying Academic Communities." *Journal of Research in Science Teaching* 32(1): 99–119.

Svinicki, Marilla D., ed. 1990. *The Changing Face of College Teaching.* New Directions for Teaching and Learning No. 42. San Francisco: Jossey-Bass.

Svinicki, Marilla D., and Nancy M. Dixon. 1987. "The Kolb Model Modified for Classroom Activities." *College Teaching* 35: 141–46.

Svinicki, Marilla D., Anastasia S. Hagen, and Debra K. Meyer. 1996. "How Research on Learning Strengthens Instruction." In *Teaching on Solid Ground: Using Scholarship to Improve Practice,* edited by R.J. Menges, M. Weimer, and Associates. San Francisco: Jossey-Bass.

Tierney, William G. 1993. *Building Communities of Difference: Higher Education in the Twenty-first Century.* Westport, Conn.: Bergin & Garvey.

Tinto, Vincent, Anne Goodsell Love, and Pat Russo. 1993. "Building Community." *Liberal Education* 79(4): 16–21.

Travis, J. 1995. *Models for Improving College Teaching: A Faculty Resource.* ASHE-ERIC Higher Education Report No. 6. Washington, D.C.: George Washington Univ., Graduate School of Education and Human Development. ED 403 811. 143 pp. MF–01; PC–06.

Treisman, Uri. 1985. "A Study of the Mathematics Performance of Black Students at the University of California–Berkeley." Doctoral dissertation, Univ. of California–Berkeley.

Tudge, Jonathan R. December 1992. "Processes and Consequences of Peer Collaboration: A Vygotskian Analysis." *Child Development* 63(6): 1364–79.

Van-Cleaf, David W., and Lawrence Schkade. 1987. "Student Teacher Learning Styles: Another Dimension of Reform." *Teacher Education and Practice* 4: 25–34.

VanOverwalle, Frank, Karine Segebarth, and Mark Goldchstein. 1989. "Improving Performance of Freshmen through Attributional Testimonies from Fellow Students." *British Journal of Educational Psychology* 59: 75–85.

Vollmer, Fred. 1986. "Why Do Men Have Higher Expectancy Than Women?" *Sex Roles* 147(8): 351–62.

von Glaserfeld, Ernst. 1995. "Constructivist Approaches to Science Teaching." In *Constructivism in Education,* edited by Leslie P. Steffe and Jerry Gale. Hillsdale, N.J.: Erlbaum.

Vygotsky, Lev. 1978. *Mind in Society: The Development of Higher Psychological Processes.* London: Harvard Univ. Press.

———. 1986. *Thought and Language.* Cambridge, Mass.: MIT Press.

Wallerstein, N. 1983. *Language and Culture in Conflict: Problem-Posing in the ESL Classroom.* Reading, Mass.: Addison-Wesley.

Watson, J.B. 1924. *Behaviorism.* New York: Norton.

Watson, Lemuel W., and Frances K. Stage. 1998. "A Conceptual Framework for Student Learning, Involvement, and Educational Gains." In *Enhancing Student Learning: Setting the Campus*

Context, edited by Frances Stage, Lemuel Watson, and Melvin Terrill. Alexandria, Va.: ACPA Media.

Weidman, John. 1989. "Undergraduate Socialization: A Conceptual Approach." In *Higher Education: Handbook of Theory and Research,* vol. 5, edited by J. Smart. New York: Agathon Press.

Weiner, Bernard. 1979. "A Theory of Motivation for Some Classroom Experiences." *Journal of Educational Psychology* 71(1): 3–25.

———. 1980. *Human Motivation.* New York: Holt, Rinehart & Winston.

———. 1986. *An Attributional Theory of Motivation and Emotion.* New York: Springer Verlag.

———. 1992. "Attributional Theories of Human Motivation." In *Human Motivation: Metaphors, Theories, and Research,* edited by B. Weiner. Newbury Park, Calif.: Sage.

Werner, Liedtke. 1977. "The Young Child as Problem Solver." *Arithmetic Teacher* 24(4): 333–38.

West, Russell F. 1982. "A Construct Validity Study of Kolb's Learning Style Types in Medical Education." *Journal of Medical Education* 57: 795–96.

Whitman, Neal A. 1988. *Peer Teaching: To Teach Is to Learn Twice.* ASHE-ERIC Higher Education Report No. 4. Washington, D.C.: Association for the Study of Higher Education. ED 305 016. 103 pp. MF–01; PC–05.

Wilhite, Stephen C. 1990. "Self-efficacy, Locus of Control, Self-assessment or Memory Ability, and Study Activities as Predictors of College Course Achievement." *Journal of Educational Psychology* 82: 696–700.

Wilkerson, LuAnn, and Wim H. Gijselaers. 1996. "Concluding Comments." In *Bringing Problem-Based Learning to Higher Education: Theory and Practice,* edited by L. Wilkerson and W. Gijselaers. New Directions for Teaching and Learning No. 68. San Francisco: Jossey-Bass.

Wilson, Timothy, and Patricia Linville. 1982. "Improving the Academic Performance of College Freshmen with Attributional Techniques." *Journal of Personality and Social Psychology* 42: 367–76.

———. 1985. "Improving the Performance of College Freshmen with Attributional Techniques." *Journal of Personality and Social Psychology* 49: 287–93.

Wingspread Group on Higher Education. 1993. *An American Imperative: Higher Expectations for Higher Education.* Racine, Wis.: Johnson Foundation.

Woolfolk, A.E., and W.K. Hoy. 1990. "Prospective Teachers' Sense of Efficacy and Beliefs about Control." *Journal of Educational Psychology* 82(1): 81–91.

Wren, Carol T., and Gail Harris-Schmidt. 1991. "Collaborative Learning in Higher Education and in Schools: A Two-tiered Approach." *Teacher Education and Special Education* 14(4): 263–71.

Zevik, E. 1994. "Masks and Mask Making: Reading and Writing a Kinesthetic Learner-Centered Approach for High-risk Students." In *Theories of Learning: Teaching for Understanding and Creativity,* edited by R. Kelder. New Paltz, N.Y.: SUNY Conference of the Institute for the Study of Postsecondary Pedagogy. ED 394 408. 232 pp. MF–01; PC–10.

Zimmerman, Barry J., and Albert Bandura. 1994. "Impact of Self-regulatory Influences on Writing Course Attainment." *American Educational Research Journal* 31(4): 845–62.

INDEX

A

academic as well as social integration in college environment
    self-efficacy relates significantly to, 28
academic learning, concepts of, 93–94
accommodators learn best in a setting that allows for concrete
    experience and active experimentation, 71
action as way to overcome problems, 61–62
active learning concept, ix
African Americans
    difference in learning styles of, 70
    female athletes' beliefs about themselves as scholars, 28
    reversing patterns of failure of, 86
Americans with Disabilities Act
    compliance with and true accessibility, 87
antecedent clues in causal attributions, 18
Aptitude Revisited, 66
assimilators learn most effectively through abstract conceptualiza-
    tion and reflective observation, 71
attribution
    framework as aspect of motivation, 7
    status of research on, 75
    style assessment test and questionnaire, 76
    theorists explain achievement behavior by people's beliefs,
        11
    theory, x, 9–21
"authentic experience," providing students with, 43

B

Bandura, Albert
    how to develop self-efficacy (1994), 86
    particular importance of structured transitions (1997), 25
    self-efficacy as basis for learning-centered college, 23
banking
    concept of learning, 54
    model as ingrained behavior, 63
behaviorist theory
    dominated psychology through much of this century, 4
    influence still evident today on college campuses, 5
Bruner, Jerome, 35, 37

C

calculus classes, reversing patterns of failure in, 86
career-related self-efficacy, 27

constructivism. *See also* social constructivism.

      learning from process of active construction of knowledge, 35

      theories of learning that emphasize active role of learners, 34

      versions of, 36–37

      views of knowledge and learning, 35–36

contexts for learning, internships, and classroom assignments as, 5–6

controllability dimension, 12

convergers most comfortable with abstract concepts and active experimentation, 70–71

critical consciousness, 56

      union of action and reflection imperative for, 61–62

critical learning, literature conducive to promoting, 80

cultural negotiation of knowledge, 39

current contextual clues in causal attributions, 18

curriculum situated in the learner's reality, 52

D

decoding a problem as goal of dialogue, 60–61

democratic dialogue in the classroom, 52

dialogue, 60–61

divergers prefer concrete experience and reflective observation, 71

      many minority students learn more easily in this manner, 72

diversity and learning styles, 72–73

domain specific

      instruments for focusing on beliefs for college students, 77

      self-efficacy is highly, 25–26

Drew's analysis of science and mathematics, 67

E

education, purpose of, 57

educational psychology focused on cognitive functioning and how people process, organize and retrieve information, 5

efficacy for general academic skills scales, 77

effort as proverbial double-edged sword

      turning against its master when failure occurs, 15

empowering learning, literature conducive to promoting, 80

enculturation, learning as a process of, 40

English as a second language. *See* ESL.

environmental control, 29

ESL (English as a second language), 62, 63

essential not to follow me in order to follow me, 64

esteem needs, 6
executive processing, 29
explicit challenging goals enhance and sustain motivation, 24

F

"factory model" classroom, 53
faculty mostly are assimilators, 71
failure attributed to stable uncontrollable causes accompanied
   by a low sense of self-efficacy, 13
failure continually attributed to external causes, 15–16
females in mathematics
        skepticism about ability eroding sense of self worth, 28–29
frameworks, criteria for selecting, 3
framing of feedback, 26
Freire, Paulo
    concept of learning, 54–55
    conceptions of learning, (1970b), focus of, 60
    difference between problem solving and problem posing,
       (1981), 59–60
    insights into learning theory, 52
    pedagogy applications to college classroom in literature, 62
    pedagogy calls for transformative relationship between
       students and teacher, 58
    problem-posing procedure for critical dialogue, 63
    theory and service learning, connections between, 89–90
    Theory of Conscientization, x, 51–64
    three fundamental components of, 52
freshman interest groups as learning community, 88
future success for high expectations
        in event of success achieved under stable conditions, 12–13

G

Gardner's (1983) theory of multiple intelligences, 65, 66, 67
    needs more research, 74
gender differences, 17
    learning styles relationship to, 71
"generative themes," 60
Gergen, social constructionism of, 37
global measures of academic success
       various measures of self-efficacy that have consistently
         demonstrated positive relationship to, 28
goal of dialogue as "decode" problem, 60–61

grading in rank order postings as detrimental to student
   achievements, 31
group learning
      triadic dimensionality of Weiner's conceptualization of
         causal attributions upheld in, 84
group work
      student resistance to, 64

H

Heider (1958)
      founding father of attribution theory, 10
      redirect attention away in explaining achievement behavior
         from how people feel to what people believe, 11
hierarchy of needs that motivates humans, 6
higher education, social constructivism in, 41
how students learn, few have studied, 1–2

I

incentive value of success, motivation described in terms of, 7
Indiana Center for Evaluation, x
Indiana University, x
instruction focus is one-sided, 2
instructor and student interaction in the social constructivist
   classroom, 43–44
intelligence and learning assumptions, 66–67
internal attributions for success
      as most powerful predictor of end-of-year measures, 19
internships and classroom assignments as contexts for learning, 5–6
"intersubjective" knowledge, 43
"intersubjectivity," 38
intransitive consciousness, 55
"intuitive guesswork," 83

K

Kelly (1955) redirect attention away from how people feel to what
   they believe, 11
key features of social constructivism, 39
knowledge and learning, social constructivism's views of, 37–40
knowledgeable other, Vygotsky's supporters stress role of, 45
"known reality," 54
Kolb's inventory of learning styles
      learning styles at college level typically measured using, 80

Kolb's learning styles, 65
> typology of, 66
> value of, 70

Kolb's theory and related research
> implications for approaches to learning, 71

L

Latino students, reversing patterns of failure of, 86

learning
> as ongoing modifications in our mental frameworks, 35
> assumption occurs in association with attending college, 1
> descriptions of importance of perceived self-efficacy in, 24
> environments conducive to self-efficacy development, 26, 30

learning-centered classroom, value for students of, 26

learning community, 83, 87–88
> common forms of, 88

learning paradigm assumptions, 2

learning styles, 69–71
> and the college classroom, 71–72
> differ according to ethnicity and cultural background, 70
> relationship to gender differences, 71
> relationship with attitudes toward education, 71
> status of research on, 75, 80–81

lecture style involving active teaching and passive learning, ix

levels of consciousness, overlapping of, 57

liberatory learning, literature conducive to promoting, 80

linked courses as learning community, 88

listening, 60

living-learning centers, 88

locus contingent on internal factors within the individual, 12

love needs, 6

low effort as cause of failure
> student expectancy of future success remains high with, 14

M

magical consciousness. *See* semiintransitivity.

mastery experiences, 26

medical schools, adoption of problem-solving learning by, 46–47

monograph, purpose of this, 2–3

motivation
> as internal process that guides behavior over time, 6
> descriptions of methods for changing, 6–7

motivational
>processes generated cognitively using self-beliefs, 24
>theories as critical in understanding behavior and
>>learning, 6

multiculturalism
>social constructivism supports a foundational tenet of, 48

multidimensional/multiattributional causality scale, 76

multiple intelligences, 67–69
>status of research into, 75, 81

multiple intelligences and college students, 69

music use in college classroom, 87

N

native semitransitive consciousness, 55–56

nonpositivistic approach to knowledge, 55

nonwestern cultures tend to emphasize field-dependence, 73

O

*Over the Ivy Walls: The Educational Mobility of Low-Income
Chicanos*, 51

P

participatory teaching formats, 52

Pedagogy of the Oppressed, 52, 56

peer
>influence power in cultivating healthy causal attributions for
>>academic outcomes, 19–20
>learning, 83
>learning technique, 45
>teaching and self-efficacy, 85–86

perceived controllability, 26

perceived probability of success, motivation described as, 7

performance, self-efficacy as strong predictor of, 29–30

personal decision making and development
>most individually focused studies concentrated on, 1

physiological needs, 6

Piaget, Jean, 35
>constructivist theories influenced by, 37

political activism, self-efficacy relate significantly to, 28

prior conceptions of ability, 26

problem-based learning
>perceived as more meaningful than conventional courses, 79
>reason why valued, 47–48

problem-posing approach to education, 59–60
problem-solving approach to education, 59
program of coordinated studies as learning community, 88
psychological theories typically associated with literature on
    college students, 4
psychology of learning, constructivism as most current theory in, 36
purpose of education, 57

R
radical constructivism, 37
range of intelligences at college level, 69
resistance to Freirian pedagogy, common areas of, 63–64
resolution of dilemmas, social constructivism's emphasis on, 43

S
safety needs, 6
"sage on the stage" concept, ix
salient explanations for outcomes range is surprisingly narrow, 11
self-actualization needs, 6
self-concept drives achievement behavior, 16
self-efficacy, 24
        academic achievement studies relating to, 27
        achievement through motivational processes, 24–25
        college classroom, 28–30
        college students, 23–32
        framework as aspect of motivation, 7
        how to develop, 86
        learning, 24–27
        predictor of performance, 29–30
        problem solving linked with ability produced largest
            gains, 18
        relate significantly to political activism, 28
        status of research on, 75, 77–78
"self-handicappers" divert attention away from low ability as
    explanation for failure, 15
semiintransitivity, 55
service learning, 83, 89
        connections with Freire's theory, 89–90
        theories of learning that can be applied to programs of, 89
Skinner (B.F.) believed in psychology goal of predicting and
    controlling human behavior, 4–5
social comparisons, 26
social constructionism of, 37

social constructivism, x, 37–40. *See also* constructivism.

    dilemmas associated with, 48–49

    learning from, 33–49

    model of college classroom, 40–43

    status of research on, 75, 78–79

social efficacy, activities that positively influence, 26–27

social engagements enabling student to participate in cultural
  practices of the discipline must be focus of classroom, 42

social interaction in learning

    constructivism charged with ignoring, 37

social learning emphasis on, 5

social persuasion, 26

social processes relationship to college students' success

    extensive work in the study of, 1

socially negotiated knowledge

    educators providing learners with conditions that
       promote, 40

sociocultural approaches, 37

somatic and emotional states, 26

specific theories of learning, status of research on, 75–76

stability as whether a cause fluctuates or remains constant, 12

structured transitions importance, 25

student

    belief about efficacy, situations that can influence, 26

    -centered learning, 36, 52

    discussion of applicability of Freire's thought to affairs of, 62

    emotions influenced by self-efficacy beliefs, 25

    interaction in social constructivist classroom, 44–45

    lives shaped by self-efficacy, 25

    self-beliefs and behavior, studies of relationship between, 29

student teachers' beliefs related to differences that could affect
  future success, 28

"success plan," 23

T

teacher's role in problem posing, 60

teacher-student relationships, 57–59

teaching

    connections with learning theory, 83–91

    English as a second language, 62, 63

    five approaches to, 83

technology

    as an approach to teaching, 83

role in college classroom, 86–87
testing modes advantage to students of particular learning styles, 71
theories of motivation, 24
transformative relationship between students and teacher, 58

U

union of action and reflection for critical consciousness, 61–62
University of California–Berkeley
      intensive mathematics workshops at, 86

V

vicarious experiences, 26
videos used in college classroom, 87
von Glaserfeld, Ernst, 35, 37
Vygotsky, Lev, 35, 37
      emphasized role of the teacher in the educative process,
         43–44
      ideas relatively untested in postsecondary education, 79
      influenced greater recognition of social influences, 37
      social constructivism draws most heavily on the work of, 38
      supporters stress role of the more knowledgeable other, 45
      theory of social learning, 63

W

Weiner's classification of underlying dimensions for causes of
  success and failure needs more work, 76

Since 1983, the Association for the Study of Higher Education (ASHE) and the Educational Resources Information Center (ERIC) Clearinghouse on Higher Education, a sponsored project of the Graduate School of Education and Human Development at The George Washington University, have cosponsored the ASHE-ERIC Higher Education Report series. This volume is the twenty-sixth overall and the ninth to be published by the Graduate School of Education and Human Development at The George Washington University.

Each monograph is the definitive analysis of a tough higher education problem, based on thorough research of pertinent literature and institutional experiences. Topics are identified by a national survey. Noted practitioners and scholars are then commissioned to write the reports, with experts providing critical reviews of each manuscript before publication.

Eight monographs (10 before 1985) in the ASHE-ERIC Higher Education Report series are published each year and are available on individual and subscription bases. To order, use the order form on the last page of this book.

Qualified persons interested in writing a monograph for the ASHE-ERIC Higher Education Report series are invited to submit a proposal to the National Advisory Board. As the preeminent literature review and issue analysis series in higher education, the Higher Education Reports are guaranteed wide dissemination and national exposure for accepted candidates. Execution of a monograph requires at least a minimal familiarity with the ERIC database, including *Resources in Education* and the current *Index to Journals in Education*. The objective of these reports is to bridge conventional wisdom with practical research. Prospective authors are strongly encouraged to call at (800) 773-3742 ext.14.

For further information, write to
ASHE-ERIC Higher Education Report Series
The George Washington University
One Dupont Circle, Suite 630
Washington, DC 20036-1183
Or phone (202) 296-2597
Toll free: (800) 773-ERIC

Write or call for a complete catalog.

Visit our Web site at **www.gwu.edu/~eriche/Reports**

ADVISORY BOARD

James Earl Davis
University of Delaware at Newark

Kenneth A. Feldman
State University of New York–Stony Brook

Kassie Freeman
Peabody College, Vanderbilt University

Susan Frost
Emory University

Kenneth P. Gonzalez
Arizona State University

Esther E. Gotlieb
West Virginia University

Philo Hutcheson
Georgia State University

J. Roderick Lauver
Planned Systems International, Inc.–Maryland

Daniel T. Layzell
MGT of America, Inc., Madison, Wisconsin

Clara M. Lovett
Northern Arizona University

Meredith Ludwig
American Association of State Colleges and Universities

Laurence R. Marcus
Rowan College

Robert Menges
Northwestern University

William McKeachie
University of Michigan

Diane E. Morrison
Centre for Curriculum, Transfer, and Technology

John A. Muffo
Virginia Polytechnic Institute and State University

Patricia H. Murrell
University of Memphis

L. Jackson Newell
University of Utah

Steven G. Olswang
University of Washington

Laura W. Perna
Frederick D. Patterson Research
  Institute of the College Fund/UNCF

R. Eugene Rice
American Association for Higher Education

Sherry Sayles-Folks
Eastern Michigan University

Jack H. Schuster
Claremont Graduate School–Center for Educational Studies

Leonard Springer
University of Wisconsin–Madison

Marilla D. Svinicki
University of Texas–Austin

David Sweet
OERI, U.S. Department of Education

Jon E. Travis
Texas A&M University

Dan W. Wheeler
University of Nebraska–Lincoln

Donald H. Wulff
University of Washington

Manta Yorke
Liverpool John Moores University

REVIEW PANEL

Richard Alfred
University of Michigan

Robert J. Barak
Iowa State Board of Regents

Alan Bayer
Virginia Polytechnic Institute and State University

John P. Bean
Indiana University–Bloomington

John M. Braxton
Peabody College, Vanderbilt University

Ellen M. Brier
Tennessee State University

Dennis Brown
University of Kansas

Patricia Carter
University of Michigan

John A. Centra
Syracuse University

Paul B. Chewning
Council for the Advancement and Support of Education

Arthur W. Chickering
Vermont College

Darrel A. Clowes
Virginia Polytechnic Institute and State University

Deborah M. DiCroce
Piedmont Virginia Community College

Dorothy E. Finnegan
The College of William & Mary

Kenneth C. Green
Claremont Graduate University

James C. Hearn
University of Georgia

Edward R. Hines
Illinois State University

Deborah Hunter
University of Vermont

Linda K. Johnsrud
University of Hawaii at Manoa

Bruce Anthony Jones
University of Missouri–Columbia

Elizabeth A. Jones
West Virginia University

Marsha V. Krotseng
State College and University Systems of West Virginia

George D. Kuh
Indiana University–Bloomington

J. Roderick Lauver
Planned Systems International, Inc.–Maryland

Daniel T. Layzell
MGT of America, Inc., Madison, Wisconsin

Patrick G. Love
Kent State University

Meredith Jane Ludwig
American Association of State Colleges and Universities

Mantha V. Mehallis
Florida Atlantic University

Toby Milton
Essex Community College

John A. Muffo
Virginia Polytechnic Institute and State University

L. Jackson Newell
Deep Springs College

Mark Oromaner
Hudson Community College

James C. Palmer
Illinois State University

Robert A. Rhoads
Michigan State University

G. Jeremiah Ryan
Quincy College

Mary Ann Danowitz Sagaria
The Ohio State University

Kathryn Nemeth Tuttle
University of Kansas

RECENT TITLES

Volume 26 ASHE-ERIC Higher Education Reports

1. Faculty Workload Studies: Perspectives, Needs, and Future Directions
   Katrina A. Meyer

2. Assessing Faculty Publication Productivity: Issues of Equity
   Elizabeth G. Creamer

3. Proclaiming and Sustaining Excellence: Assessment as a Faculty Role
   Karen Maitland Schilling and Karl L. Schilling

Volume 25 ASHE-ERIC Higher Education Reports

1. A Culture for Academic Excellence: Implementing the Quality Principles in Higher Education
   Jann E. Freed, Marie R. Klugman, and Jonathan D. Fife

2. From Discipline to Development: Rethinking Student Conduct in Higher Education
   Michael Dannells

3. Academic Controversy: Enriching College Instruction through Intellectual Conflict
   David W. Johnson, Roger T. Johnson, and Karl A. Smith

4. Higher Education Leadership: Analyzing the Gender Gap
   Luba Chliwniak

5. The Virtual Campus: Technology and Reform in Higher Education
   Gerald C. Van Dusen

6. Early Intervention Programs: Opening the Door to Higher Education
   Robert H. Fenske, Christine A. Geranios, Jonathan E. Keller, and David E. Moore

7. The Vitality of Senior Faculty Members: Snow on the Roof—Fire in the Furnace
   Carole J. Bland and William H. Bergquist

8. A National Review of Scholastic Achievement in General Education: How Are We Doing and Why Should We Care?
   Steven J. Osterlind

Volume 24 ASHE-ERIC Higher Education Reports

1. Tenure, Promotion, and Reappointment: Legal and Administrative Implications
   Benjamin Baez and John A. Centra

2. Taking Teaching Seriously: Meeting the Challenge of Instructional Improvement
   Michael B. Paulsen and Kenneth A. Feldman

3. Empowering the Faculty: Mentoring Redirected and Renewed
   Gaye Luna and Deborah L. Cullen

4. Enhancing Student Learning: Intellectual, Social, and Emotional Integration
   Anne Goodsell Love and Patrick G. Love

5. Benchmarking in Higher Education: Adapting Best Practices to Improve Quality
   Jeffrey W. Alstete

6. Models for Improving College Teaching: A Faculty Resource
   Jon E. Travis

7. Experiential Learning in Higher Education: Linking Classroom and Community
   Jeffrey A. Cantor

8. Successful Faculty Development and Evaluation: The Complete Teaching Portfolio
   John P. Murray

Volume 23 ASHE-ERIC Higher Education Reports

1. The Advisory Committee Advantage: Creating an Effective Strategy for Programmatic Improvement
   Lee Teitel

2. Collaborative Peer Review: The Role of Faculty in Improving College Teaching
   Larry Keig and Michael D. Waggoner

3. Prices, Productivity, and Investment: Assessing Financial Strategies in Higher Education
   Edward P. St. John

4. The Development Officer in Higher Education: Toward an Understanding of the Role
   Michael J. Worth and James W. Asp II

5. Measuring Up: The Promises and Pitfalls of Performance Indicators in Higher Education
   Gerald Gaither, Brian P. Nedwek, and John E. Neal

6. A New Alliance: Continuous Quality and Classroom Effectiveness
   Mimi Wolverton

7. Redesigning Higher Education: Producing Dramatic Gains in Student Learning
   Lion F. Gardiner

8. Student Learning outside the Classroom: Transcending Artificial Boundaries
   George D. Kuh, Katie Branch Douglas, Jon P. Lund, and Jackie Ramin-Gyurnek

Volume 22 ASHE-ERIC Higher Education Reports

1. The Department Chair: New Roles, Responsibilities, and Challenges
   Alan T. Seagren, John W. Creswell, and Daniel W. Wheeler

2. Sexual Harassment in Higher Education: From Conflict to Community
   Robert O. Riggs, Patricia H. Murrell, and JoAnne C. Cutting

3. Chicanos in Higher Education: Issues and Dilemmas for the 21st Century
   Adalberto Aguirre, Jr., and Ruben O. Martinez

4. Academic Freedom in American Higher Education: Rights, Responsibilities, and Limitations
   Robert K. Poch

5. Making Sense of the Dollars: The Costs and Uses of Faculty Compensation
   Kathryn M. Moore and Marilyn J. Amey

6. Enhancing Promotion, Tenure, and Beyond: Faculty Socialization as a Cultural Process
   William G. Tierney and Robert A. Rhoads

7. New Perspectives for Student Affairs Professionals: Evolving Realities, Responsibilities, and Roles
   Peter H. Garland and Thomas W. Grace

8. Turning Teaching into Learning: The Role of Student Responsibility in the Collegiate Experience
   Todd M. Davis and Patricia Hillman Murrell

Quantity   **Amount**

_____Please begin my subscription to the current year's
ASHE-ERIC Higher Education Reports at $120.00, over
33% off the cover price, starting with Report 1.   _____

_____Please send a complete set of Volume ___ *ASHE-ERIC
Higher Education Reports* at $120.00, over 33% off the
cover price.   _____

Individual reports are available for $24.00 and include the cost of shipping and handling.

SHIPPING POLICY:

- Books are sent UPS Ground or equivalent. For faster delivery, call for charges.
- Alaska, Hawaii, U.S. Territories, and Foreign Countries, please call for shipping information.
- Order will be shipped within 24 hours after receipt of request.
- Orders of 10 or more books, call for shipping information.

All prices shown are subject to change.

Returns: No cash refunds—credit will be applied to future orders.

PLEASE SEND ME THE FOLLOWING REPORTS:

Quantity	Volume/No.	Title	Amount

Please check one of the following:

☐ Check enclosed, payable to GW-ERIC.   **Subtotal:**

☐ Purchase order attached.   **Less Discount:**

☐ Charge my credit card indicated below:

   ☐ Visa   ☐ MasterCard   **Total Due:**

Expiration Date_____

Name_____

Title_____

Institution _____

Address_____

City _____ State _____ Zip_____

Phone _____ Fax _____Telex_____

Signature _____ Date_____

SEND ALL ORDERS TO: ASHE-ERIC Higher Education Reports Series
The George Washington University
One Dupont Cir., Ste. 630, Washington, DC 20036-1183
Phone: (202) 296-2597 ext. 13
Toll-free: (800) 773-ERIC ext. 13
FAX: (202) 452-1844
URL: www.gwu.edu/~eriche/Reports

DATE DUE
